CONNECTING: BEYOND THE NAME TAG

HOW TO BECOME A POWER NETWORKER WHILE BUILDING MUTUALLY BENEFICIAL RELATIONSHIPS

WILLIAM M. SALEEBEY, PH.D.

LOS ANGELES

Connecting: Beyond the Name Tag

By William M. Saleebey, Ph.D.

Published by Believe Publishing

Believe Publishing
401 S. Citrus Avenue
Los Angeles, CA 90036
www.BelievePublishing.net

Book web site: www.ConnectingBook.com

For speaking engagements or to contact the author: DrBillSaleebey@gmail.com

Cover design by Bemis Balkind
Interior layout by Jonathan Gullery

First Edition, November 2009

ISBN: 978-0-9842396-0-3

Cataloging-in-Publication\Data is on file with the Library of Congress

Includes bibliographic references and index

1.   Business networks
2.   Career development
3.   Interpersonal communication
4.   Business development
5.   Business communication
6.   Social networks
7.   Personal growth
I. Title

Printed in the United States of America
10 9 8 7 6 5 4 3 2

CONTENTS

PART 5
APPENDICES 137

*A book designed to assist business professionals
in expanding their professional and personal networks
to develop referrals, resources, ideas, and contacts.
Readers will increase their sphere of influence,
enhancing personal development,
and career advancement.*

DEDICATION

To my parents Bill and Selma Saleebey, who taught me
by example how to connect with others. They were the
ultimate networkers and built their business by
establishing genuine relationships.

TESTIMONIALS

"Dr. Bill Saleebey has captured the real essence of networking that the most effective approach is to adopt it as a lifestyle. He has removed any negative stigmas about networking by reinforcing the benefits of sharing, first and foremost, and not asking for anything in return. This book is a must read for both the novice and experienced networker."

Davis R. Blaine, Chairman, The Mentor Group; Managing Director, ProVisors

"Dr. Saleebey has revealed the psychology and process of relationship building for business and life. He has taken the mystery out of networking and laid out a practical framework for building sustainable relationships of trust, friendship, support, and sharing. Whether one is selling products or services, building a circle of trusted advisors and resources, or cultivating referral relationships, this book is for you."

Gordon Gregory, Chairman and Managing Director, Mosaic Capital LLC
Managing Director, ProVisors

"Brilliant! Superbly written, packed with insight and practical tips. Dr. Saleebey taps his immense gifts for relating to others with years of success in the business world to bring to life the many nuances of networking. With example after example, he elaborates how networking not only enriches our lives but enhances the lives of everyone around us. In an easy, conversational style, he underscores a simple truth: our need to belong is met tenfold through effective networking skills. This is a highly comprehensive and reader-friendly work."

Louis F. Markert, Ph.D., Instructor, UCLA Extension

"Bill's observations regarding the power of relationships and reciprocation have created a wonderful guide for anyone who's interested in growing their business through networking."

Bunni Dybnis, Director, LivHome

"Dr. Saleebey's book provides a great overview of the importance of networking. It also shows the steps to achieving success in networking, and this is reinforced by his real life examples and how they have been successful for others. A good read if someone wants to build their networking circle and skills."

Mark Davidson, Underwriter, Arden Realty

"Networking is as much science as it is art. It involves focus, intention, organization and pragmatism. Dr. Bill Saleebey is focused, intentional, organized and pragmatic. Read this book. Keep it by your desk. Red-line the hints. You'll be better than you thought possible."

Mike Altman, Principal, Simon Altman & Kabaker Inc.

"The insights that Dr. Saleebey draws from the networking process truly shows that he participates in that process."

Larry Whittet, C.E.O., American Relocation & Logistics

"If there's a strength William Saleebey best typifies, and he does typify many strengths, it's networking. This guy connects with more people on more levels in a year than most people meet in a lifetime and it works. Read the book! You will not be disappointed."

Marc Swan, Rehabilitation Counselor, Aetna Insurance

"Bill takes the generic world of 'networking' and drills down to the psychological fundamentals that will help you identify people who will help you build effective business and personal networks."

Barbara Wasserman, Principal, Wave2 Communications

"*Connecting* is informative and fun to read. Based on the author's extensive experiences and intimate knowledge of the subject matter, the book is replete with well-chosen examples and helpful common-sense advice. The writing style is clear, direct and conversational, combined with a practical approach to the art of relationship-building that makes the book extremely accessible. I highly recommend it."

Michael Friedberg, Partner, Friedberg & Trombi

"I've read *Connecting* several times and each time gain more tips, ideas, insight, and wisdom into what has become a fun and innovative experience for me, networking. By following Dr. Bill's suggestions, people remember me better, warm up to me more easily and are more willing to assist me. I found more complete and useful information in this book than I've read by any author."

Michele Hurtubise, Certified Facility Manager

"Saleebey's timely book is indispensable not only as a primer on how to use networking groups for business advantage, but also for how to network as a part of creating social communities. It provides a clear picture of various networking opportunities for professionals."

Katherine Wolff, Attorney

"*Connecting* is an extremely helpful guide and reference for business people who need to network. Dr. Saleebey's experience, wisdom and humor transcend this very readable book that anyone in business should read."

Scott O. Harris, Ph.D., Principal, Harris Sherman Consulting Group

"Dr. Saleebey's book not only thoroughly explores its subject matter but adds additional insight by examining the individual and psychological aspects of networking in a way that has never been done before. This allows the reader to explore the possibilities for enhancing their life and career through networking as well as understanding their personal relationships in the process."

Wendy Robin Weir, Masters in Psychology, Licensed Acupuncturist

ACKNOWLEDGMENTS

Writing a book is truly a team effort. I learned an enormous amount about teamwork and collaboration when I was teaching a course called Teamwork, Collaboration, and Conflict Resolution for University of Phoenix. I couldn't have written and published this book alone. I needed help, sought it, and received it from a variety of people. It was also a great form of networking.

First and foremost I want to recognize my son Billy Saleebey for encouraging me to write the book in the first place. He was developing my web site and blog, and said, "Dad, you should really write a book on networking." He inspired me, did a number of readings and editing, managed the publication of the book, and was always there for me when I needed ideas or motivation. He's my brightest star.

My copy editor, Nomi Kleinmuntz, brought attention to detail and inspiration to the project. Sanjay Nambiar of Tengo Communications provided expert organizational skills and sage advice. He was a great team member, always supportive and on the mark.

Gordon Gregory and Davis Blaine, Managing Directors of ProVisors, were extremely supportive of the book, and opened the door to many ProVisors members who agreed to be interviewed. They include Steve Martini, Bob Weinberg, Judy Jernudd, Mark Goulston, Richard Sinopoli, David Ackert, Eric Bruck, Bunni Dybnis, Scott Harris, Rick Rhoads, and Andrew Apfelberg. Chuck Hurewitz, my attorney, provided invaluable feedback to make this a better book and was a true trusted advisor.

Randy Sheinbein, Managing Director of Bruin Professionals, has been a seminal force in my networking career. I thank him deeply for welcoming me into BP, for many business referrals, for publishing my article on the front page of the web site, and for giving me a platform to speak on several occasions. He truly believes in me. A number of BP members were helpful as readers or interviewees: Ken Chong, Scott Spiro, Katherine Wolff, and Mark Davidson.

Larry Whittet, CEO of American Relocation & Logistics, has been my most consistent and enduring mentor. He has provided me with a career, always respected my opinions, and encouraged and supported my networking activities. Larry is a friend and a boss, and a great example of how business mixes with our personal life.

Marc Swan, Wendy Weir, and David MacGillivray read early drafts of the manuscript and made valuable comments and corrections which I heeded. Dr. Lou Markert, Michele Hurtubise, and Mike Altman did an outstanding job of editing and were supportive of the project.

Judy Moore is unquestionably the most important person in my life. She's my "significant other," my roommate, and my best friend. She has tolerated my rigorous networking schedule, even when it has meant very early mornings on numerous occasions. She asks where I'm going at such an ungodly time, listens to my response, "another networking meeting," and rolls over and goes back to sleep.

ABOUT THE AUTHOR

Dr. William Saleebey is the foremost expert on the psychological dimensions of personal and business networking. He received his Ph.D. in Education with a specialization in Counseling from UCLA in 1980. He also holds an M.S. in Counseling from California State University, Hayward, and a B.A. in Psychology from UCLA.

Dr. Saleebey has been a college professor at a number of universities since 1973, including California State University, Los Angeles, University of San Francisco, UCLA Extension, Chabot College, and University of Phoenix. His expertise is quite broad. He has taught courses in General Psychology, Counselor Education, Applied Business, Learning Skills, Sales, and Team Building. He's currently lecturing throughout the United States on Business Networking. Dr. Saleebey has written two books, *Study Skills for Success* and *Sell Yourself*. *Study Skills for Success* was developed as course material for the Study Skills Seminar, an educational program he developed for high school and college students in 1978. *Sell Yourself* was the result of over 25 years experience in sales as Regional Manager, Corporate Relocations, American Relocation & Logistics, a commercial relocation organization and agent for Mayflower Transit, where he has been a high producer for many years.

He has also written numerous articles on a wide range of topics, including: business networking, commercial relocation, and group process. His doctoral dissertation, "Educational Problems of Samoan Migrants," was based on his year as a counselor and professor in American Samoa. This research was anthropological in nature, and grounded him in the understanding of multicultural factors in human behavior.

In addition to his professorial experience, he has been a professional public speaker for the Association of Legal Administrators, Bruin Professionals, ProVisors, LivHome, Coldwell Banker, IFMA, Institute of Real Estate Management, Renaissance Executive Forums, and numerous service clubs and chambers of commerce. He delivered a commencement keynote address for

Associated Technical College. His presentations are lively, timely, relevant, and filled with useful information. He performed stand-up comedy for several years, and injects humor into all of his presentations.

Dr. Saleebey has been involved in business and social networking for over twenty-five years. Originally he utilized this process for his own business development in commercial relocation sales and marketing. As time passed, he became deeply involved not only as a participant, but as an organizer of networking groups. He has served in a variety of executive positions, and has become a recognized thought leader and expert in the field. He's currently on the Board of Directors of Bruin Professionals, a UCLA alumni group, and is an active member of ProVisors, Building Owners and Managers Association, and International Facility Management Association.

Dr. William Saleebey is a dynamic and engaging personality, capable of captivating audiences nationally. This book is the culmination of many years of experience, research and interviews with a wide variety of professionals. It combines the results of extensive observations of a variety of networking styles and venues that have demonstrable effectiveness in yielding referrals, resources, and increased commerce.

INTRODUCTION

My educational and professional background is unusual. I earned a B.S. in Psychology, an M.S. in Counseling, and a Ph.D. in Education with a specialization in Counseling and a minor in Theater Arts. I've been teaching, primarily at the university level, since 1973. My teaching experience is broad, with stints in Psychology, Counselor Education, Applied Psychology, Business, Communication, Sales Training, Learning Skills, Group Process, Team Building, and Ethics. I've taught courses and seminars throughout the United States and American Samoa. My latest foray has been into the field of business networking, which combines all of the above disciplines. I've authored two books, *Study Skills for Success* and *Sell Yourself,* as well as numerous articles on topics such as: time management, effective teaching techniques, commercial relocation, and business networking.

I bring a psychological perspective and background to bear on this topic which makes my approach unique. This book addresses the psychological aspects of networking and the interpersonal factors that cause us to connect and build mutually beneficial relationships. The focus is on individual differences, group dynamics, and other psychological factors not sufficiently emphasized by previous authors. My specific perspective is variously that of a psychologist, educator, researcher, and participant-observer in business networking endeavors as a salesperson and business development specialist.

My sales career began in 1982 and has involved all aspects of transportation, specifically in commercial relocation. My job involves developing leads and referrals for businesses that are expanding, contracting, consolidating, and making use of relocation services, storage, and related consultation. My primary responsibility is business development. I've provided all of those services, been a top salesperson in the Mayflower transportation system, and have coordinated over 3,500 business relocations.

In 1998 I was approached by a commercial real estate broker whom I had met in a "lead exchange" business networking group that centered around relocations. He told me about a Los Angeles based business networking group called All Cities. It consisted of about two hundred business professionals including a high percentage of attorneys, accountants, bankers, and financial professionals. I was a commercial relocation consultant/salesperson, so I figured "Why not?" Little did I know how obsessed I would become with "business networking," let alone that it would become a legitimate skill set about which I would write and speak. I stayed in that group, where I could "guest" at different chapter meetings, for about three years. During that period, coincidentally, I met another commercial real estate broker, who, like me, was an alumnus of UCLA. He was launching a new UCLA alumni professional networking group to be called Bruin Professionals (BP). I've been involved in the development of BP from its inception, assisting in the launching of various chapters. I attend all current chapter meetings monthly and serve as Speaker Chair of one chapter. In addition, I'm a member of several relocation-specific professional organizations such as Building Owners and Managers Association (BOMA) and International Facility Management Association (IFMA). What started as a suggestion in 1998 has become a way of business life for me and led to a lucrative referral business generating millions in revenue for my company.

After a few years I discontinued my involvement with All Cities and joined a larger networking group called ProVisors. ProVisors has over 1,300 members in California, mainly top level professionals from a variety of fields such as law, accounting, banking, insurance, financial planning, architecture, real estate, entertainment, and consulting. ProVisors has numerous chapters and industry affinity groups that meet monthly as well as frequent social networking events, which provide many opportunities for socializing and making connections. Additionally, ProVisors expands on the concept of networking to emphasize collaboration among trusted advisors and other respected professionals to better serve the needs of their respective clients.

Bruin Professionals and ProVisors utilize a "troika" or "mini" concept (developed by ProVisors) as a follow-up for general membership meetings. There is first a large chapter meeting (twenty to forty people), with introductions, occasional speakers, and a section called "Needs, Deals, Wants, and Testimonials," when individual members thank and publicly acknowledge others for referrals or a job well done, state business or personal needs, and talk about deals that have been consummated as a direct result of involvement with others in the group. Then all members of the large group are arbitrarily broken up into smaller groups of 3 or 4 people for a follow-up breakfast, lunch, or dinner at another time (preferably within a month, or before the next large group meeting). It's in these smaller groups that people really get to know each other and learn about what is on the *back of the business card* (this consists of more personal information that's not directly related to business). The small group meetings are often devoted to discussing in more detail about our job, and things about our personal lives including topics such as travel, children, and hobbies. The small group experience of the "troika" allows a deeper relationship to develop. It also provides a better opportunity to communicate for those who are introverts or have difficulty speaking in front of a large group. Additionally, the discussion in large groups is sometimes superficial and general. There's even a difference in the dynamics within groups of two, three, or four people. Some people tend to dominate the discussion in all groups, but the smaller group at least gives the possibility for changing that tendency. You can learn more about people in the small group setting, such as how they collaborate with others, weigh in on various topics and listen to others because smaller groups allow for more intimate discussion.

In over ten years in several different groups I've observed and experienced a dramatic increase not only in my own personal network, but also in referral business, and I have been exposed to a world of people I didn't know before. These networking groups (and there are many others like the ones I participate in) represent a kind of business "sub culture," and it's not uncommon to see some of the same people in the different organizations. For example, many of my Bruin Professionals colleagues are also active members of ProVisors.

It should be noted that this book is based primarily on my personal experiences and observations of many others' experiences with business networking in the greater Los Angeles area of California. My psychological education and training, coupled with the interviews and case studies of others offer a wide perspective on the topic. These ideas and principles can be applied to many other regions and demographics. Certain psychological and group dynamic principles apply across a wide spectrum of society while others are more specific to certain demographic groups.

We often wear NAME TAGS in life. They only provide basic information, such as our name and company. This book gets us *beyond* that name tag to the person and the connections we make.

***The term "tweet" stems from its use on the micro blogging platform Twitter. A

tweet is a short message (140 characters or less) that you post on the site. For inspira-
tion, and as an example of online networking, I have included a selection of "tweets"
that I have made over time.

> **Networking really begins after the handshakes,**
> **small talk, smiles and exchange of business cards.**
> **You need to get beyond the name tag.**

PART 1

GETTING STARTED

WHAT IS NETWORKING?

A BRIEF HISTORY OF BUSINESS NETWORKING

BUSINESS networking is not new. People have been involved in networking groups, formal and informal, for as long as there has been commerce. In years past it might have been church, a service organization like Rotary or Kiwanis, neighborhood gatherings, or trade organizations that provided the source for networking. In the 70s and 80s the most prominent business networking group was Le Tip. In Le Tip, which has chapters in locations throughout the United States, it is necessary to bring at least one "lead" to share with another member of your chapter. This isn't really networking in the true sense, but better described as a lead exchange. What seems to be happening now is an explosion of formal networking groups of all types, plus the influx of social networking sites like LinkedIn, Facebook, Twitter, and Plaxo. People who are in the business of being "rainmakers" or business development specialists have realized it's imperative to network in order to keep their businesses alive and vibrant. The days of waiting for the phone to ring are over for many firms. Professionals such as attorneys and accountants now need to get out from behind their desks and drum up business for their firms. Many such individuals need to develop the skills discussed in this book in order to be successful in building relationships and networks.

Modern networking has drawn individuals who traditionally have had enough referral business without networking. Professionals like lawyers and accountants have been called on to develop new business as well as to find additional resources to refer to for matters or cases outside of their area of specialization. Many professionals use networking more for making rather than receiving referrals. They find reliable resources to refer matters outside their area of expertise. Gordon Gregory, Managing Director of ProVisors, defines networking as "the resourcing and collaboration of trusted advisors and respected professionals."

In his timely book *Endless Referrals (2005),* Bob Burg provides an excellent definition of networking. He states, "Networking is the cultivating of mutually beneficial, give-and-take, win-win relationships." He emphasizes the fact that rather than being dependent or independent, we're all interdependent. All things being equal, people do business with and refer business to, people they know, like, and trust. It's not only who you know, but who knows you and what you do that leads you to increased referrals and business.

There are many aspects and levels of networking, from the basic form of finding work and connections to more sophisticated forms of deal making and brokering. You'll see where your personal networking form and style are, and then you can make the appropriate application for maximum benefit. Factors like geography, culture, specific profession, and status will also have a significant impact on how you actually apply these ideas. Networking opportunities occur frequently, often in places where you might not expect them. Keep your eyes and ears open and be ready for them. View your sphere of influence as a group of social circles and consider ways to manage them, enlarge them, and juggle them. Consider yourself a fisherman casting a net, many nets, and remember that you may catch more and different varieties in your nets than what you originally intended.

Many factors determine the form and function of your networking program. You might be looking for more direct business referrals for your business. In other cases, you might be looking for people to whom to refer business or matters outside of your area of expertise. It's useful to set intentions and to have specific goals, but it's also important to be open to factors and variables not part of your original goals for networking.

In some cases networking starts with a business intention and leads to lifelong friendships. I've found that networking provides not only business referrals (giving and receiving) but also some very good friendships that I had neither anticipated nor expected. There have never been more potential opportunities or channels than there are today. Social media, for example, provide the potential of instantaneous worldwide networking which was not available until the advent of the Internet.

> **Paul Revere was one of the earliest American networkers. He knew many people, and many people knew him. The British wish it were otherwise.**

WHY SHOULD YOU READ THIS BOOK?

This book discusses the real nature of personal and business relationships and how to build them. You'll understand how to form mutually beneficial relationships, how to develop them, and how to nurture them and make them fruitful. Whether you're new to sales or entrepreneurship or a veteran, you'll gain an increased understanding of the networking process and how to benefit from it.

Networking has many facets. It can be something you do almost unconsciously without any effort or specific intention. You might network because you're told by a supervisor or trainer, "You have to build your network." It might be something you do because you're curious about people or like people. You might even join an organization and get involved in activities on a volunteer basis without the expressed intention of networking. In her book *The Power of Networking*, Sheila Savar suggests networking can provide a quicker and more efficient way of connecting with others than other methods, whether you want simply to expand your network or find a job.

If you want to learn about every major aspect of networking and how to become a more effective networker, this book is for you! You'll learn about different types of people, types of groups, and forms of networking. Though some other authors on this topic eschew the term *networking*, I'll use it in this book for its basic utility and appropriateness. If you're interested in people and how they form groups, keep reading with an open mind.

The examples throughout the book are based on observations and interviews with a variety of people. They demonstrate many different networking styles and strategies. From them you'll get many useful ideas, and develop your own plan and accompanying techniques.

This book will motivate and inspire you to develop, nurture, and maintain relationships that are not only enjoyable, but have a tangible value for increasing your business. It provides various examples of where, when, and why to network. You can join professional networking groups, service clubs, alumni associations, chambers of commerce, trade organizations, athletic teams or church groups, or seek networking almost anywhere. Networking is a holistic approach to building relationships, incorporating social media, face-to-face encounters, and a way of life.

> **People join networking groups for a variety of reasons: to get referrals, find referral sources, professional development, and fun.**

NETWORKING BASICS

SHOWING UP

THERE'S no substitute for "showing up." In order to be effective doing face-to-face networking, you've got to consistently attend meetings and functions, and then follow up. Others get familiar with you and get to know you better when you do that. Since I'm a member of several groups I've had the occasion to notice some people are more VISIBLE than others. It could be the quality of their personality, their charisma or their like-ability. Whatever the case, some members are more memorable than others. One primary reason is consistency of attendance. Punctuality and staying around until the end of the meeting are also important. Arrive early so you can greet everyone who attends the meeting. The more time people see you and experience your presence, the better it is for your networking success. I constantly hear people say they should guest more and attend more consistently, but it's the action of doing so that matters. It is really a combination of attendance and personality, in addition to the clarity of your statements, that lead to being memorable, and ultimately to increased referrals and commerce.

The goal is to establish a consistent and positive visibility that leaves an enduring imprint on others. You want to become memorable in a positive way.

Consistency is vital. If you don't show up consistently and your competitors do, then they will be remembered more than you. The more people see you, interact with you, like you, and know what you do, the more chance you'll get referrals or do some kind of business. Visibility is crucial to success in networking.

Someone once said to me, after seeing me at many networking meetings over a number of years, "You really don't need to come to meetings anymore because everyone already knows you and what you do." I was taken aback, then commented that I enjoyed the camaraderie and I would soon be forgotten if I didn't continue to attend on a regular basis. Showing up is also a tangible sign of my commitment to others and to the process.

An apt example of the opposite is seen in networking groups where some people don't actually show up, but send in their business card so they can be included in troikas. It's not the same as actually attending, and some regular attendees resent the fact that those people are not showing up but still want the benefits of attending. Taking such shortcuts may be excusable in emergencies, but as a routine practice, it's soon seen as an aspect of one's character and lower level of commitment.

> **Networking Tip - Attend your networking group regularly; show up early and stay late.**

GEOGRAPHICS AND NETWORKING

Effective networking usually requires your physical presence. You can only be effective by showing up. For example, I can be really effective in promoting my commercial relocation business in the greater Los Angeles area. The majority of my business originates from Los Angeles County. Few people know me well outside of that domain. Fortunately for me, Los Angeles County has well over eight million people. But in areas as close to Los Angeles County as Orange County (the O.C) and Ventura County, I have far fewer real contacts who have actually met me in person. Geography plays a key role in personal networking (face-to-face). For me, the specific business areas of Downtown Los Angeles, Century City, Westwood, Beverly Hills, Hollywood, Culver City, and the greater San Fernando and San Gabriel Valley (in California) are strong. People there know me, know my face, and I get numerous referrals in those regions. This works for me primarily because of the kind of business I'm in. Other types of business may require you to expand your network outside of your geographic area, necessitating travel or heavy online networking.

It should be emphasized that there are significant regional and cultural differences in networking styles. The information contained in this book would definitely apply in other medium-sized to large cities in the United States. However, there would be some variation in certain techniques in small towns, among different cultures, and abroad.

Although networking and building strong relationships can occur in ways other than face-to-face, there's no substitute for spending quality time with others. Sharing a meal, having coffee, taking a walk, going to a sporting event, or having cocktails are all viable ways for strengthening bonds.

I've observed that certain individuals have very strong relationships in one geographic area and are virtually unknown in others. Someone's name will be mentioned prominently in Downtown Los Angeles, but they might have no name recognition in other regions. Other people are known in a wider area due to things like media coverage, publications, or other forms of notoriety.

3

CREATING A POSITIVE IMPRESSION

HOW TO MAKE A GOOD FIRST IMPRESSION

It has been said that you only have one opportunity to make a first impression. There are many things others might notice about you when they first meet you that comprise that impression. For example, punctuality is very important to some people. To those people, if you're late you might already have one strike against you. Any way you inconvenience someone else will probably lead to a negative first impression. Another example is clothing attire. If you go to a business meeting clad in short pants and a polo shirt you'll create a certain impression, regardless of the reason you're dressed that way.

The concept of first impression has both a positive and negative aspect. We're either favorably impressed (positive) or unfavorably impressed (negative). A genuine smile, a positive demeanor, a firm handshake, good eye contact, and general affability will usually make a positive first impression. Conversely, over-seriousness, negativity, hyperactivity, and not being personable lead to a neutral or negative first impression.

There's no single way to make a good first impression because people are all so different. If you mention traffic, some people will consider that topic to be complaining (and thus negative), while others will agree with you and share their experiences with traffic. You might talk about a film you just saw and liked, and if the other person liked that film then your impression of them might be positive. But if they didn't like the film, they might judge you negatively. A lot depends on tolerance of individual differences. Some people tend to only associate with like-minded people (other Republicans, other Methodists, other dog lovers), while others have a much more diverse group of friends and associates. You don't have to agree with a person on all subjects to make a connection. It's easier to make diverse connections if you're tolerant of opinions different from your own and maintain an open minded attitude.

First impressions often are based on others' personal appearance and hygiene. But once again, the impression depends on the expectations and personal taste of the other person. If they expect you to wear a business suit and you appear in shorts and sandals, you'll create a negative impression. In his book *Click,* George Fraser (2008) emphasizes the importance of how you present yourself physically. He refers to it as "creating an air of distinction." Though you might not be a "clothes horse" or interested in fashion, it never hurts your image to always dress as sharp as possible. The best rule of thumb is to dress appropriately for each situation and also to have something unique about your attire. There's a gentleman in my networking group who always wears a bow tie. It makes him unique in that group because he's usually the only one who wears a bow tie. It's part of his personal *brand.* To fully understand this concept, you need to consider people's preconceptions, biases, preferences, and expectations. Impressions are not facts, but opinions based on our expectations. We might have a negative first impression of someone, and not realize that their mother just died and they're in a state of extreme sadness, which we perceive as negativity.

Impression formation can be quite psychologically complex. People can remind us of others whom we might like or dislike. Physical attractiveness (or unattractiveness), foreign accents, size, age, and attire are among the factors that can influence the formation of our impressions of others. It can be useful to check our initial impressions or assumptions with others if we doubt our own judgment. This will enable us to confirm or check our impressions and perceptions.

Obviously, the goal is to create a positive first impression. We control a lot about how people form impressions of us. It helps to be consistently courteous, respectful, and agreeable. Show up on time, smile, listen attentively, and respond appropriately. When you have a negative first impression of others, be willing to revise that impression based on new information. Give people a second chance, because we all have bad days and bad experiences that can affect our moods.

LIKEABILITY AND GENUINENESS

It's a well accepted fact that people want to be around and do business with people they like. A necessary characteristic for success in networking is likeability. Those who smile, are good listeners, and are positive about life tend to have more people in their sphere of influence. It might begin with a handshake and a smile but it goes deeper than that. Why do we like some people more than others? There are a multitude of reasons, and some of them are intangible.

Don't underestimate a simple and genuine smile. A smile denotes a welcoming attitude and a certain measure of happiness. It's vital to call people by name. It might seem trivial, but it makes a difference when you learn and remember people's names. Generally people appreciate it when others learn and remember their name, the nature of their work, and other pertinent facts about them. Likeability is akin to charm, and sometimes we don't know why we like some people more than others — we just do.

A likable, genuine person is easy to be around. They listen and understand us, like to have a good time, remember things that we tell them, and CONNECT. The quality of likeability is necessary for building lots of harmonious relationships but not enough to sustain them. The quality of our work must support likeability. There are cases when I know two or more individuals who do the same thing. Perhaps all of them are equally competent, but one of them is simply more likable, and as a result, will tend to get more of my referrals. Simply stated, we tend to do business more with people we like than those we don't like or feel neutral about!

Another component of likeability is *warmth.* We perceive some people as being warm and approachable. Warmth is a combination of genuineness, being personable, and connecting emotionally on a personal level. This quality could include hugging, touching, and other displays of appropriate affection. All of these factors lead to an increased comfort level. It's really a matter of being *personable,* and not exclusively focused on business. Warm people genuinely care about others and are interested in their lives.

The key to connecting with people is to establish rapport. Rapport is a level of comfort between people that's gained through a number of contacts and is characterized by increased familiarity. It's the result of a positive connection, and takes a certain amount of time to establish. As we come to know and trust one another we're able to be on a more casual, informal basis. As the rapport is further developed and solidified it's easier and more natural to ask for referrals, advice, and assistance. Another term to describe this phenomenon is "chemistry."

Likable people are usually nonjudgmental and not argumentative. They don't push their point of view. They're reasonable, fair, agreeable, accommodating, flexible, and kind. They usually have a high level of empathy and compassion for others. In sum, likeable people like others and others like them. They radiate and are connected to a positive field of energy, a tightly woven web that researchers have conclusively demonstrated can affect the DNA structure — that's how deep positive feelings go! There are numerous factors that make people likeable. You might like someone who always shows a genuine interest in you or makes you feel comfortable.

> **No matter how you slice it, you have to be likable
> to succeed in networking.
> You can't "e-mail it in" or hide behind
> your computer screen.**

NETWORKING EXAMPLES: EXPLANATION

The networking examples appearing throughout the book under the various headings are based on actual people I've known, interviewed, and observed in the course of my business and personal networking. They're intended to illustrate various principles and aspects of networking. Some represent the essence of successful networking experiences, some are in the middle, and others are examples of negative experiences. There is and always will be a huge range of networking experience, from the positive and financially rewarding to negative and uncomfortable situations. Hopefully the positive ones will be your experience, but nothing is perfect or guaranteed. I want to present a realistic picture of what networking is about.

As you read each example try to apply the related principles to your situation. Even if the example may be different from something that you have experienced, try to utilize the principle to add to your repertoire of effective networking tools.

The essence of my method is to apply the most useful and relevant principles and techniques, not necessarily all of them or in a particular way. It is a flexible method and not something to be memorized and applied in a rigid manner. THE ESSENCE OF EFFECTIVE NETWORKING IS GENUINENESS.

NETWORKING EXAMPLE: UNCLE BUCKY

Uncle Bucky is a very popular member of a networking group in which I'm involved. Bucky is about 70 years old and well known and highly regarded within the group. He's very pleasant and warm, and always calls people by name. He often uses the slang version of the name, where Bill is Billy, Bob is Bobby (or Bobalu), and Joe is Joey. He's so well liked that no one seems to mind his use of nicknames. I'm using him as an example because of his enormous likeability. He has a masterful way of connecting and clicking with people. He often uses humorous Yiddish expressions. The expressions are especially resonant with a predominantly Jewish group, and probably wouldn't work at all in another demographic group. His style has allowed him to connect more quickly and deeply with others. He really "fits in" with this population.

Bucky makes people feel comfortable. He's warm and genuine, obviously comfortable with himself. When you're talking to him, he makes you feel important and special. He remembers what you do and what you last talked about. He's always helpful and tries to make referrals.

There's another key element of Uncle Bucky's style, and that's his generosity. He always insists on picking up the tab at restaurants. He owns and operates a lending organization. He's financially successful, and his generosity is legendary among members of this networking organization. He's a "class act," and his likeability is instrumental in securing business deals for his company. Others in the networking group know him, like him, and trust him. Consequently, business deals are referred to him on a regular basis.

LEARNING AND USING PEOPLE'S NAMES

It's critical to call people by name! Though it might seem like a small thing, people respond much more to people who learn and *remember* their name. Pay attention to a person's name exactly as they state it. Don't use nicknames or shortened versions until you really get to know someone (or have status within a group like Uncle Bucky). The best way to remember someone's name is to use it frequently at first until it's fixed in your memory.

There's a substantial difference between saying "Hello" and "Hello, Bob." (Bob especially will notice the difference.) Being called by name personalizes the relationship and indicates that the other person remembers us. Use mnemonic devices or whatever it takes to commit people's names to memory. Ask yourself the question: how do you feel differently about people who always call you by name and those who don't. There's a difference, though it may be on more of an unconscious level.

In his book *The Relationship Edge,* Jerry Acuff (2007) emphasizes the importance of learning people's names to move up their "relationship pyramid." He contends the best way to get people to call you by name (thus moving up his pyramid) is to use theirs on a consistent basis. If you use others' names most will feel obligated to learn and use yours. Acuff's pyramid concept is intriguing and valuable. It ranges from:

The goal, obviously, is to get people to that last and highest level through honesty, keeping commitments, reliability, trustworthiness, and a proven track record. It takes time to build rapport and business relationships. Acuff warns that it's easier to move down the pyramid than up, and that when people truly value the relationship with us, then we can make mistakes and they are more likely to tolerate it than when we're at the lower levels.

Personally, I'm more likely to forgive tardiness with someone who has been punctual in the past than with someone I'm meeting for the first time. When someone who I'm meeting for the first time keeps me waiting more than a few minutes, especially when I'm busy, I expect them to acknowledge and explain their tardiness. I'm usually understanding in regard to situations beyond someone's control, like a traffic accident or car breakdown. But if a person is late and seemingly disrespectful of my schedule, then they create a negative first impression.

WHAT DO YOU SAY AFTER YOU SAY HELLO?

Usually networking begins with the sometimes awkward first meeting, where you might see someone's name tag, introduce yourself, and say "Hello, I'm Bill Saleebey" (at least that's what I would say). So, what do you say after you say hello? An age-old question, to be sure. For some extroverts and people who have the "gift of gab" this process is easy and seamless. Some people are very comfortable with what might be called "small talk." Others are uncomfortable, tongue-tied, and hopeful the other person will lead and carry the conversation. There are no simple answers for this situation, but it does get easier the more we do it. You might start with simple questions like, "Is this your first meeting?" or try to discover something you have in common with the other person. In any event, you'll need to make some conversation and should listen for cues about the other person's interests, occupation, and hobbies. They might say something about a recent vacation or something that is happening at their place of employment.

The more people you know in a group the easier it is to do this kind of open networking. I've noticed that the more people I know in a group the less effort it takes to mix and mingle. People come up to me, know me, and we often have a history and can pick up a conversation we had started at a previous meeting.

It's useful to set some type of goal for each event prior to attending, if appropriate. Concentrate on the people with whom you're speaking. Ask them questions about what they do, and probe further if you don't initially understand. You need to identify people with whom you want additional contact. In his very useful book *Endless Referrals,* Bob Burg (2005) suggests that the key question you should ask others is, **"How can I know if someone I'm speaking to is a good prospect for you?"** Answers will guide your listening so you can be of maximum assistance to the many people you meet. I strongly recommend you approach networking with the attitude of GIVING rather than taking. Think about what you can possibly do or say to help other people become more successful. If you do that on a consistent basis, I guarantee you'll get things back in abundance. Too many people are overly concerned about what they're getting and not what they can give.

It's vital always to be thinking of the various ways in which you might be helpful to others! You might make an introduction, be a trusted advisor, or make an enthusiastic referral. Never miss an opportunity to do the right thing. Consistently practice acts of kindness and generosity.

It should be noted that the open networking/mingling stage is not where business is usually done. It's like a warm-up to the meeting, the introductions, and the small group follow-up meetings. However, it's a common starting point, and the place where we make and form first impressions. Some people really enjoy this aspect of networking which is often heavy on "small talk." The more you go to networking events, and the more people you already know in those groups, the easier and less awkward is this process.

THE ELEVATOR SPEECH

In many business networking group meetings there's a moment when each member gives what has been referred to as an elevator speech. The concept comes from the hypothetical scenario of being in an elevator with someone and then having a minute or less to answer the question, "What do you do for work?" The goal is for each person to do their introduction in a manner that's clear, understandable, interesting, memorable, and simple.

As an example, mine goes something like this: "Good morning, I'm Dr. Bill Saleebey, and I'm Regional Manager, Corporate Relocations for American Relocation and Logistics, a full service moving and storage company. I have a doctorate in Education, and they call me 'Dr. Move,' because I educate our clients on how to keep their productivity up when they move their offices. I coordinate and manage commercial relocations. I recently moved a large law firm from one building to another in Century City. They closed at noon on Friday and by 8 a.m. on Monday their new office was completely operational, with no loss of productivity or billable hours. So any time you or someone you know is relocating their business, either within their current building, locally, or around the country, give me a call. No job is too small or too large. For any relocation needs, contact me. Bill Saleebey, American Relocation & Logistics."

Some people can describe exactly what they do in a clear and memorable way, and others are either unclear, rambling, hazy, or sound like everyone else. You can either come up with a script that you memorize and present the same way each time or vary the speech from time to time. If you're unsure about the effectiveness of your elevator speech, ask for feedback from others.

One issue for the elevator speech is the length. Depending on the meeting or situation you might have 30 seconds to 2 minutes or even more. Try to keep to the limit. Work on being confident and clear, and speaking in a strong voice. Practice your elevator speech whether it's memorized verbatim or changes a bit each time. After your elevator speech, members of the audience should know your name and company, exactly what you do, what a good referral to you would be, and if time permits, a specific example of the service you provide.

It helps if you use humor or something to make yourself unique. You can also use examples to embellish your points. Our introduction provides others with a snapshot, a quick impression of who we are and what we do. It should project confidence, passion, clarity, and a positive attitude.

You want your introduction to differentiate you. What makes you and your occupation unique? What exactly do you do? What would a great referral look like? Why should someone give a referral to you instead of someone else? You should present yourself as welcoming and approachable. It should be businesslike but not overly serious.

NETWORKING EXAMPLE: THE HELPFUL GUY

Joe is a loan broker whose position allows him to secure financing for individuals with mediocre or bad credit. There are a couple of things noteworthy about Joe. First of all, he has developed a memorable and unique "elevator speech," which is not only very funny, but so catchy that members of many chapters of ProVisors have memorized it and mimic Joe when he does it. Secondly, he's extremely helpful, and always reads the "Needs and Wants" section of the e-mail newsletter and takes the time to connect people. People remember him for that and refer business to him accordingly. Once I was taking a trip to his home town of Boston, and asked for some ideas for restaurants and hotels. He took the time from his busy schedule to draw me a map and pointed out restaurants, hotels, and places of interest. Joe is not only very likable, but memorable and extremely helpful. He is someone people want to help because he's so helpful himself.

It should be mentioned that though the elevator speech is a potential form of advertising for you, it's probably not the most important part of the networking process. In large groups it's difficult to remember what everyone says and what their specialty is. Savar (2008) argues against the term "elevator pitch" and recommends that a more appropriate term is "company position statement." My position is that the term elevator speech, like the term "networking," is less important than what it signifies. We know what we're doing, and it doesn't really matter what we call it. We might nitpick over terminology, but the real activity is the important thing.

CHARISMA AND BEING MEMORABLE

Some people have charisma. They sparkle and shine, and others are drawn to them. John F. Kennedy, Martin Luther King, Ronald Reagan, Bill Clinton, Oprah Winfrey, and Barack Obama all have charisma in abundance. Charismatic people are memorable. They're usually charming and often handsome, beautiful, or in some way physically striking. They might have physical stature or a nicely shaped body. There's something about them, an aura, that makes them stand out.

In networking, some people are more memorable than others. They're like magnets for other people. In some cases they're funny, in others they're captivating story tellers or natural leaders. They have confidence, but sometimes mask any trace of ego with humility. Memorable people have a unique ability to get the attention of many people. These people stand out in a crowd and often have a dominant personality. Charisma is about the public self, and it explains the success of some who have it. However, there must be substance behind the public image, such as the ability to follow through and get things done.

The concept of charisma explains why certain individuals are more popular than others. In some cases a charismatic personality is coupled with status, position within a group, and success. It could be the quality of a person's voice, their self-confidence, experience, or a combination of other factors that make someone charismatic and thus memorable. Aligning yourself with charismatic people can assist you in your networking activities.

**"There are two ways of spreading light:
to be the candle or the mirror that reflects it."
— Edith Wharton**

4

CONNECTING

CAPITALIZING ON COMMONALITIES

WHEN you're talking to others, whether in a formal networking context or not, you'll find things in common with them. It could be where you went to school, your ethnicity, playing a particular sport or game, having children the same age, or virtually anything. In order to make connections you need to capitalize on common experiences, interests, and skills. For example, if you find out that someone attended the same university as you did, make sure to let them know you went there also. If the other person shows excitement about this shared experience, then you can ask pertinent questions to determine if the commonalities run deeper, such as having the same professors or major. If you find out there's strong common ground then you can discuss it more and expand the connection. You do have to be careful because not everyone has an equal degree of connection to or affinity for their past. I went to UCLA and received two degrees from there. In addition, I'm deeply involved in Bruin Professionals as a charter member, and on the Board of Directors, Speaker Chair for a chapter. So when I meet someone who went to UCLA, I express genuine interest and excitement and often invite them to Bruin Professionals meetings or events. They may or may not share my degree of connection to UCLA.

> **Effective networkers ask open ended questions to uncover others' passions. Once they have struck gold, they keep digging.**

Commonalities serve as an opener, and if we want to connect we need to jump on them and use them as a means to deepen our connections. There are countless ways we can find a common ground. Sometimes we find it accidentally and other times we might learn something about someone and then bring up the topic. The goal is to find the possible synergy and to "click" with others.

Here are some examples of possible topics of potential commonality where we can connect and click with others:

- Children
- Animals
- Gardening
- Games/Sports
- Travel
- Films
- Music
- Current Events
- Schools
- T.V. Shows
- Birthplace
- Neighborhoods
- Age
- Food
- Foreign Language
- Books
- People in Common
- Birth Order
- Fraternal Organizations
- Religion
- Politics
- Hobbies
- Retirement

- How We Spend Time
- Investments

The important thing is not necessarily YOUR interest in any of the above topics, but finding common ground and others' interest in them. For example, you might be very focused on retirement but the thirty year old to whom you're speaking is probably not. The more *versatile* you are in your range of discussion topics, the more people you can reach.

> **Networking Tip - Find out what you have in common with others to connect, not what you disagree with or find different.**

EMPATHY

Empathy can be defined as the ability to accurately relate and understand the world of another. It can be summed up in the following phrases, "I know exactly how you must feel," "I completely understand your situation," or "I totally get it." People with high levels of empathy tend to connect with others. Empathy usually flows from similar experiences such as losing a sale, a difficult client, divorce, or even the death of a family member. When we communicate with others, and we feel we do understand and relate to what they're going through, we should communicate that. If a speaker talks to me about having a receptive (or unreceptive) audience, I can relate to that from my vast experience as a professor. The broader our experience and the better we listen, the more often we can share empathic responses. People like talking to others who understand exactly what they're experiencing.

When we accurately empathize with another person, it leads to an increased comfort level. People might have a tendency to share more personal information with us. Sometimes they reveal more than they originally intended about emotional situations having to do with their children, their marriages, or even their personal failures or crises. There's a certain risk in being overly empathic because some people will take advantage of our perceptiveness and sensitivity.

People tend to open up around empathic people and share personal matters that they wouldn't ordinarily discuss. In a business setting you can decide how much you want to respond (or not respond) empathically to others' feelings. You must be careful to be attuned to what others are experiencing, NOT just to what you're experiencing. Empathy implies an *accurate* reading of another's feelings and experiences.

Empathy is an important quality to possess. It should lead to us being less self-centered in our business lives. When I first started in sales I was less concerned with what my prospective customer might be going through than with whether or not I made "the sale." Over time I learned it was important to always listen intently and to tune in to that person's situation and needs. For example, if someone tells me they're concerned about being late because their child is sick, I can relate to that. Or they might talk about a broken marriage, a death, a beloved animal, or a crop of peaches that got frozen. In all of these examples, it's your response that demonstrates an understanding of the others' situation and feelings related to it. Empathy will make you more successful in all aspects of your life. Support groups such as bereavement groups or recovery groups are great examples of how empathy can help people cope with loss or difficulty by associating with others who have similar experiences.

NETWORKING EXAMPLE: FINDING "COMMON GROUND"

This was a case that began with a relationship with Lou. I met Lou at a networking group and saw him a number of times at both large meetings and "troikas." At one point, he used my moving services to do a home move. At that point, I met his wife, Cathy, who is a travel agent. I was planning a trip to Italy and asked Cathy if she could assist me. She did, and has on subsequent European vacations. I not only got a referral, but so did she. Additionally, I found another connection with Lou when we discovered that our birthdays were two days apart and that we were born in the same year. What started as a weak connection developed in a few different and unexpected ways. Through our networking group, which encouraged business referrals, a business relationship developed. Although I haven't yet given Lou a direct business referral, we have developed a personal relationship and friendship. We've had dinner together as couples, and talked about our children, travel, and our other interests and hobbies.

Networking is greatly enhanced by life experience, which leads to empathy, which in turn leads to stronger personal connections and business.

Relationships often develop in unique and unexpected ways. It's useful to be flexible in your thinking. In many cases the referrals might *seem* to be one-sided, but as you have increased contact you might find different ways in which you can assist each other. It isn't always business, and not always a direct referral. It could be an introduction, trusted advice, or ideas. It's often the *attitude of helpfulness* that develops and nurtures relationships. Sometimes it's directly related to business referrals and commerce and other times it might be something totally unrelated to business. As you find more things in common with others, you'll often learn more about them and eventually be able to refer business or make appropriate introductions.

5

COMMUNICATION

THE IMPORTANCE OF LISTENING AND REMEMBERING

THE vital importance of good, active listening skills is central to your success in networking and building relationships! People like to meet people who are attentive and interested listeners. Active listening is crucial to one's overall success in life and business. It's also important to remember what people tell us. In this way you can build on the conversations you have had with people rather than always starting from scratch, asking the same questions, or forgetting key data people provide to you.

Listening should occur with a genuine interest in getting to know more about a person. Don't just go through the motions of listening, but actually focus, pay attention, and follow the conversation. One useful technique is to repeat what has been said in a different way, to lock it into our memory. Focus your full attention on the person you're speaking with. People like to feel understood and memorable, and usually like it when we remember key things about them, such as the names of their children, their hobbies, or where they went to school. Make a strong effort to be a superb listener and remember what you hear. Active listening skills communicate an attitude of caring and concern.

Good listeners have developed the virtue of patience, and when we talk to them we don't feel rushed or minimized. I notice that when I'm around someone who has strong listening skills, and is genuinely interested in me and my story, it's easier for me to communicate. I don't have to fight to get my point across. Strong listening skills involve asking open-ended questions, and *really* listening intently to the full answer. Jiddhu Krishnamurti, the Indian philosopher, stated it well: "When you're listening to somebody, completely, attentively, then you're listening not only to the words, but also to the feeling of what is being conveyed, to the whole of it, not part of it."

It's vitally important to stay intently focused in conversation, and not to get distracted by external factors or thoughts. Turn off the mobile phone or other electronic devices, and remain in the moment with the person with whom you're speaking. Try hard not to become distracted, and choose locations to talk that have minimal ambient noise.

Additionally, avoid the tendency to brag or to impress others. Don't hold people captive to your stories. Conversation is a give and take between and among people. Avoid the urge to dominate conversations. People like others who are good listeners and those who make them feel interesting and important.

People love to talk about themselves. Allow this to happen, encourage it through great listening habits, and you'll be truly appreciated. Remember, you have two ears and one mouth, and use them in that proportion.

> **Networking tip - Don't ask for referrals or leads until you build a relationship.
> Listen with openness and genuine interest.**

LEVELS OF COMMUNICATION

There are different levels of communication and different depths of relationships. On one end of the spectrum, there's no connection or even a negative feeling. On the other end is deep, almost telepathic friendship and love. Most business relationships are somewhere in between these extremes. Some people don't want business relationships to get too personal or intimate. Some want deeper relationships but don't know how and when to cultivate them. There are a number of things you can do to enhance the deeper levels of interpersonal communication if you want them.

They are as follows:

- Listen attentively and actively.
- Respond to deeply felt statements with sensitivity.
- Show empathy for others.
- Remember what people tell you, especially things that are repeated.
- Pay attention to the other person.
- Concentrate on what they're saying.
- Make your own comments clear and understandable.
- Ask open-ended (rather than yes/no) questions to allow others to express themselves more fully.
- Establish deeper connections if others seem open to them.
- Treat personal and confidential information respectfully.

The real key is to meet people at their level. Business communication typically starts impersonal but can shift to deeper levels due to circumstances. You could be in the middle of a business conversation when the other person suddenly mentions they are upset because they're getting a divorce. If they seem like they want to discuss the matter then you have a choice about how much you engage them on the topic. In other cases you yourself might talk about personal matters and disclose something about yourself not related to business. Self-disclosure can serve to deepen levels of communication. It could be something very personal, like an admission of an addiction, or something else a bit less personal. When appropriate (or if others self-disclose), it's a useful way to get closer to them. There are situational, cultural, and regional boundaries of communication. Some people would be quite comfortable and natural talking about a serious and intimate medical procedure, while others would never discuss such a matter in a "business" setting. The important point to be grasped here is that deeper levels of communication are potentially valuable and relationship-changing, but they're not for everyone or every situation. For example, discussing the details of a recent medical procedure at a lunch meeting might be TMI (too much information).

In most business settings, people talk about (you guessed it) business. This is fine and normal. However, this can become boring and repetitious. There are only so many ways you can ask, "How's business?" One way to build rapport is to discuss more personal issues, which personalize us in the eyes of others. When people find out that your daughter is getting married or that you're getting a new dog, they can use that additional personal information to forge a deeper, more personal relationship with you.

> **Networking is mostly about different levels and types of communication. It is finding the right balance of speaking and listening.**

FINDING PASSION IN ONESELF AND OTHERS

As we listen intently to others we'll find an area that they're passionate about in their work or private lives. It could be an athletic activity, music, hobbies, common interests, their children or grandchildren, or travel. When you hit on that "hot button" it's wise to listen actively and encourage that line of discussion. People appreciate it when others are genuinely interested in the important things in their lives. When you enter someone's office, observe the pictures and plaques on their walls. They often give a clue to what's really important to the person, such as their children, animals, hobbies or vacation areas. Ask questions to determine areas of keen interest, and listen carefully to the responses. Once you learn that someone loves mountain climbing it's useful to ask about that in subsequent meetings.

Don't merely memorize a list of things about the other person that you read in their biography or online profile. For example, let's say you've heard someone likes dogs. Ask them specifically about that interest and learn not only which breeds they like but even the names of their own dogs. The inquiry must be based on genuine interest and curiosity. People can usually discern the difference between insincere comments and genuine curiosity and interest. It isn't hard to find something that interests you about another person.

People brighten up when they are talking about something about which they're passionate. There's a palpable rise in their energy level and enthusiasm. By the same token, we get more excited when we're talking about something we really love. For example, I'm an avid Scrabble player. I love the game, play it competitively, and am interested in its various nuances. When I mention I play frequently, a person can either not show additional interest, ask probing questions, or have a similar interest. If by chance I find someone who also plays competitively then I might try to set up a game. I've already done that with a few fellow networkers, and though the Scrabble game is primary we also have the opportunity to talk about business. When you're paying close attention to another person, you'll be able to determine when they're talking about a subject that has deep meaning to them. They get excited and animated. These are ideal times to deepen the level of communication from superficial topics to more meaningful ones.

George Kahn belongs to ProVisors. His day job is that of a mortgage loan broker. However, his real passion is being a jazz pianist. He actively promotes his concerts and various gigs, and is known in ProVisors as "the jazz guy" as much as "the loan guy." Jazz is his passion, and a great way to connect with him. However, through people getting to know him from his concerts, he can also develop his loan business. If someone can add value to your network, go to events they invite you to.

Don't be afraid to express your passion; it will draw people to you. Conversely, look and listen for the passion in others, and encourage them to speak about things they're passionate about. Too many business people have tried to be neutral and have come across as bland and uninteresting. As Joseph Campbell teaches us, " Follow your bliss."

It's your passion (and that of others) that enables you to make an easy connection. Pay close attention to others, especially when they become animated. These are ideal times to make a true connection with another person. Allow yourself to express the things that are *really* important to you. This is what makes you unique, and allows others to relate to you on more meaningful levels. The more you share of yourself with others, the more opportunities you give for them to relate to you.

> **The more you get to know others and what they do, the more you can help them and they can help you. That is networking in its essence.**

NONVERBAL COMMUNICATION

What we say is important. What we do may be more important. Our many forms of nonverbal communication have a powerful effect on how people perceive us. Nonverbal communication accounts for a significant percentage of human communication. Our posture, facial expressions, hand and arm gestures, the clothes we wear, the car we drive, and the tonality we use (how we say things) in many cases may be more important than what we actually say.

A smile (or frown) is significant in how people receive us. Eye contact is also a major contributor to our communication package. When you approach someone, the way you move can have an impact on how you're perceived and received. Nonverbal communication also encompasses the study of *proxemics*, or body space. How close do we get to someone when we're talking to them? Where do we sit? How long do we hold someone's hand when we shake hands? Do we touch people? Do we hug members of the opposite sex (or same sex)? Personal distance refers to the actual distance we feel comfortable having between us and another person. We probably want to be very close physically to people we love and are intimate with, but not necessarily with business associates we're meeting for the first time. We probably wouldn't sit right next to someone we don't know in a restaurant booth. But we might do so with a date we really like and to whom we're attracted. In networking situations, it's useful to understand how comfortable others are with our proximity to them. For example, if we move closer to a person and they keep retreating, they're likely uncomfortable with our proximity. Be aware of others' personal space and comfort zones.

Sometimes when we describe our experience with others, we talk about exactly what is said word for word. But just as often we notice and remark on a *feeling or sense* about another person. The way they moved, how they said something (tonality), the way they looked at us, a good feeling, or a bad feeling all had some effect on us. These are all part of nonverbal communication. For example, someone's use of strong smelling perfume might influence the way we react to them. The consequences might be positive or negative depending on the setting or situation.

Do others face you and lean forward as you listen to them? Are they shaking your hand and looking over your shoulder to find the person they really want to meet? Do people roll their eyes when you complain about things? Do they nod their head in agreement when you make a controversial statement? Are they looking at a clock or their watch while you're talking? These examples relate to attentiveness and interest. The ideal scenario is to communicate nonverbally that we're fully attentive and engaged with the person to whom we're speaking and not preoccupied with something else. We communicate with our body language, facial expressions, and in many other nonverbal ways. Observe others carefully, in addition to listening to them, to determine if their words match their nonverbal communication.

There's another interesting aspect of nonverbal communication that's known as *objectics*. This refers to attire, jewelry, body piercing, tattoos, and colognes or perfumes. They're all part of how we present ourselves. We don't expect an investment banker to have a Bugs Bunny tattoo on his neck. Nor would we expect a rock musician to wear a conservative business suit for a performance. A Sunday school teacher probably wouldn't show any cleavage, but a Hollywood starlet might. One time I went to a meeting at the offices of MTV wearing a coat and tie. My host leaned over to me and said, "Take off the tie here. We're less formal." It's important to know your surroundings and the norms so that you can act and dress appropriately.

Pay increased attention to how people move, their facial expressions, what they wear, and especially how they say things. You'll learn to read people better and increase your chances of having fulfilling relationships and business success. A focus on nonverbal communication will teach you a lot about people's hidden values and agendas.

People at networking mixers often form a circle when speaking to one another (say in a group of four people). Sometimes that circle is very tight and closed to any possible newcomers. This group is communicating nonverbally that they're a closed group ("four's company, anyone else is a crowd"). A member of another small group might establish eye contact with someone seeking to enter their circle and widen the circle to include the fifth ("the more the merrier"). In both cases, nonverbal communication influenced behavior.

A great example of nonverbal communication was in the 2008 United States presidential election. President Barack Obama consistently displayed calmness and confidence, even under pressure. Conversely, John McCain often came across as angry, wooden, and cranky. There's no question that much of Obama's nonverbal behavior won over the American voters, while McCain's raised doubts about his suitability to lead.

LINEAR, SEQUENTIAL INFORMATION PROCESSORS VS. RANDOM THINKERS

This concept refers to the ways in which we typically process and communicate information. On one end of the continuum are linear, sequential information processors. These people like to think and speak in a step-by-step, detailed and sequential manner. They tend to be methodical and detailed, and they like things orderly. Random thinkers, on the other extreme, often skip from idea to idea, not necessarily logically or orderly. The latter type is often impatient with the style and approach of more linear thinkers. These different types usually have correspondingly different styles of interpersonal communication. There is, of course, is a wide range between the purely sequential and the purely random thinker.

This variation in how we process information explains why we communicate better with some people than with others. Some like to tell a story chronologically, totally in sequence. The more random thinker might explain things in terms of "feel" or "vibe" rather than specific or logical ideas. On the other hand, the sequential processor likes to complete the details of whatever it is they're speaking about. Lawyers typically think and speak differently from artists, and politicians express themselves differently than poets.

It's useful to be versatile in your thinking and communication style. When you're dealing with a person who wants all "the facts," that's what you should give them. On the other hand, some people are just looking for general information and a "feel" for what's happening. If we want a lot of detail and just get an overview, we might be dissatisfied with the conversation. There are a couple of ways to determine whether or not the person to whom we're speaking wants all of the details from start to finish or the information summarized "in a nutshell." We can ask them in advance of telling our story, read their facial expressions, or interrupt our monologue to get appropriate feedback.

When speaking with someone who has a different communication style than ours, we can let them know at the beginning of a discussion that we either want "just the facts" or "all of the details." If a person is going on and on and you find yourself annoyed or bored, you can politely interrupt at a pause in the conversation and tactfully move them along in the discussion. Conversely, when speaking with someone who's merely providing general impressions, you can press for additional details.

By being observant you'll learn to read body language like shifting in one's seat, rolling of the eyes, or looking at one's watch. Remember that what you say is important, but how you say it and your body language may be even more important. Pay attention and keep your eyes and ears open for all of the possible nonverbal cues and signs.

PART 2

GUIDING PRINCIPLES
FOR NETWORKING

NETWORKING CHOICES

PERSONAL, BUSINESS, OR BOTH

In the process of business networking the question arises: do we establish a personal relationship first or just start exchanging business referrals and professional services? Every situation is different. In some cases the personal relationship precedes the business one. You might know someone from coaching youth soccer together and not find out until later what they do for work. At that point, if the relationship is sufficiently developed, then it might be appropriate to broach the subject of business exchanges. This can begin with the simple exchange of business cards. In other cases such as a business networking meeting, you'll likely just dive into a business relationship and referral sharing.

It's not suggested that you prematurely exchange business referrals with people you don't know or trust. Perhaps we hear from a variety of sources that someone does outstanding work. Their stellar reputation is an important determinant of making a referral. If we know someone, like them, and know they do excellent work then we're more likely to refer them. We may ask the question, "What's in it for me?" In other words, what are we getting in return for our referral? I strongly suggest you focus on giving, and if you give generously and frequently, referrals will come back to you in abundance.

Sports and other games are great opportunities for having social interaction that may include a business component. Many organizations have golf tournaments, tennis tournaments, or other types of games and competition. Sign up and have a good time. Get to know others and be a positive person, a cheerleader, someone whom others like to be around. There are plenty of opportunities for pure business networking. Some people are more inclined to share business referrals and advice after they get to know others in a social setting. In fact, in some cultures and subcultures it's expected that personal interaction and pleasantries are prerequisites to conducting any business.

In his book *The Referral of a Lifetime,* Tim Templeton (2005) suggests there are four basic personality types that relate to business. These represent basic tendencies rather than absolutes. They are as follows:

- Relational-Relational — This person is almost exclusively interested in relationships, and business is secondary to them.
- Relational-Business — This person starts with the relationship (personal things), and once that has been established, develops a strategy to securing business.
- Business-Relational — This person begins with a business-like approach, and develops the relationship secondarily.
- Business-Business — This person is all business, though they will be cordial; for this person the only way to justify the value of a relationship is that it yields a business benefit or value.

Templeton encourages people to accept their basic personality type or style and to be observant of the styles of others. For example, when dealing with a Relational-Relational person, it's better not to push the business aspect initially. Conversely, when dealing with a Business-Business type, it's better to focus immediately on business.

Be attuned to cues that might hint at which aspect is more prominent or important to others, the personal or business. The interplay between these two factors is complex, and there's a lot of overlap between them. Acuff's approach rests on this notion of relationship building and the time it takes. It's not a quick fix or something on which you can take short cuts. We deepen relationships over time through numerous contacts, by sharing personal information and by developing trust and caring, which leads to sharing.

In my book *Sell Yourself: A Unique and Effective Approach to Selling Products, Services, and Ideas,* I emphasize the critical importance of establishing rapport with potential clients. Rapport is a comfortable state shared by two people that grows out of knowing and liking one another. It's a genuine connection on a personal level. The best way to develop rapport with others is to deepen levels of conversation beyond the superficial. In developing rapport we recognize each other as trusted and unique. Once we have established and developed rapport with another we feel more comfortable asking direct questions. We don't have rapport with strangers but probably have a lot of it with our spouse. As we develop a deepening rapport with others we develop that relationship. This makes it easier to do business.

> **Networking Question - Should you cast wide net in networking, or join one organization and go deep? Breadth or depth? The answer is both.**

BREADTH OR DEPTH

Whenever we're around people, whether at a networking meeting, mixer, or social event, the question arises as to how long we talk to each person and when to break away and "mingle." The traditional approach emphasizes breadth, a kind of "how many business cards did you get" mentality. Though it's usually advisable to speak to more than one person at a networking event, it's not always advantageous to mingle too quickly or frequently. There are benefits to be gained from a deeper approach, where you spend considerable time getting to know one or two people well, rather than jumping too quickly from person to person.

I favor the latter approach at this stage in my career and my leadership roles and active participation within the various groups. As I get to know more people and have a wider network, I tend to focus on one person and deepen that relationship. I address all of my energy and undivided attention toward a particular person and don't worry about meeting everyone else. The type of networking I've been talking about is NOT like "speed dating," where you only have a minute or so to judge a person (and be judged). On the other hand, there are many times when you do need to excuse yourself to "mingle," but that decision might involve numerous factors. There are credible arguments for a breadth or depth approach, and it ultimately comes down to personal preference and time avail-ability. Ideally, there will be a mix of breadth and depth.

Related to this concept is the notion of *quality* versus *quantity*. How wide are you casting your net? Are you selective in terms of which events you attend? There's a wide spectrum of possible behavior, from a very targeted and specific "networking program" with specific activities, to a more spontaneous and intuitive approach to networking. Almost anyone could be a referral source for my business, while other businesses are much more specific and limited.

The decision of *breadth* (meeting a lot of people) versus *depth* (spending more time with one person or a few people) becomes easier with experience. Common courtesy comes into play, and often there are natural breaks or lulls in conversation that will help you determine how long you spend with people. Some people take a while to warm up and if we rush them we may not get the full value of our time with them. Continue to pay attention to this issue and modify your approach to see what works best for you.

When you meet a lot of people, the time you meet them can be very impor-tant. *Primacy* and *recency* are related issues. Primacy refers to the first contact or first person you meet who does a particular thing or is in a certain category (like a personal injury attorney or tax audit accountant). For example, primacy would be your first job. Recency refers to the most recent contact of a particular category. If you meet a lot of financial planners, you might best remember the last one you met. We might then give a referral to the most recent person of a particular category. What this shows us is that we need to keep our name and face in front of people so they don't forget us.

Overall, the depth approach (more time with one or fewer people) is espe-cially useful with someone of high potential value. For example, I'll spend more time with a commercial real estate broker because they're more likely to give me a valuable direct referral to a company that is relocating.

> **There is a big difference between getting list of leads and building deeper relationships to gain enthusiastic referrals; latter is better.**

NETWORKING EXAMPLE: TARGETED NETWORKING

Richard is a financial planner whose networking is almost exclusively related to his university alumni group. He's active in the Alumni Association and the alumni business networking group. His company hosts a chapter of the networking group, which gives him added visibility. He is in effect the "home team." In addition, he's an ex-athlete, avid sports fan, and attends many athletic events. He has developed some fruitful business relationships. Unlike a "shotgun" approach which emphasizes breadth, Richard's is based on focus and depth. He's a loyal UCLA alumnus and has benefited from putting most of his "eggs" in that "basket."

Although his networking activities are mostly limited to this alumni organization, his leadership position allows him to derive maximal benefit from them. He attends many events within one large institution. His high profile through leadership has yielded him numerous referrals and a stellar reputation within those groups.

Richard has done several specific things to attain his position and status within this alumni organization. He hosts the group, he's the leader of the group, he's warm and welcoming, and he has built a few very strong referral relationships which are continually referenced during the "testimonial and thank you" segment of the meeting.

There's another factor related to intense involvement in a group, which I'll refer as the "true believer" factor. A "true believer" is someone who becomes overly zealous in a particular group and has an intense loyalty to that group, club or organization. Perhaps that person is a fanatic about an aspect of a group, such as the *athletics* of a college alumni organization. For example, there is one member of my alumni group who always wears UCLA clothing, talks about sports, and is a member of other alumni clubs and groups. This enthusiasm endears him to others who have similar feelings about the university.

You can be successful with or without an extreme loyalty or dedication to an organization. However, you can maximize your leverage within a group by becoming a highly involved and participating member of that group. For example, there might be many people who attend a given church, but few who are perceived as staunch and devout members such as the ushers, the breakfast committee, or the treasurer. The more involved members maximize the benefits of belonging to any organization. They're seen, heard, and remembered.

PART OF YOUR JOB OR A DISTRACTION?

For some people networking is a distraction, an annoyance, or something they don't seem to have enough time to do. For others it's an integral part of their business routine. In some cases networking is a central activity or even part of your job description. For example, if your job is in business development or sales then networking could likely be the main job focus. There's a huge variation in how much time and energy people spend networking, making and nurturing connections, and attending social events. This depends on both the nature of your position and on personal preference. If you want to benefit from networking, at the bare minimum you have to be highly present at the events you attend. Turn off the cell phone, listen attentively, and participate fully.

For anyone whose job is primarily in business development, networking should be seen as critical. Everyone must assess the amount of time and effort that can be allotted to networking activities, as well as discern which activities are not critical. Don't wait until you need contacts to begin networking. As motivational writer Harvey Mackay would say, "Dig your well before you're thirsty."

Treat networking as a long-term tool to build relationships that are intrinsically enjoyable and financially rewarding. Have fun in the process. You'll make new friends with some unlikely people; you'll build your network of business associates and friends and become more valuable to the people around you. You'll also learn much about various professions and positions. I've learned an incredible amount about law, insurance, and mergers and acquisitions since I've been actively networking. Networking is about developing business, but there are many other unexpected benefits and intangible outcomes from the process. Regardless of your actual job, networking will provide timely knowledge, resources, and expertise, and will increase your overall effectiveness.

A major determinant of where you place networking in your activities is the nature of your position. Closely related to this factor is whether you perform the actual services or outsource them to others. For example, if you're a writer who does all of the writing for which you market, then your networking activities might decrease when you're on a deadline or in the midst of a writing project. Another example is an attorney whose performance is partially evaluated on the basis of "billable hours." In this case, the attorney might not want to spend as much time networking because it might decrease the possibility of attaining those hours.

For some people networking is a means to the end of securing more refer-rals, more business, or a job. They network to achieve one of those goals. For others like myself, networking is enjoyable and an end in itself. I enjoy meeting new people, getting to know them, and building lasting relationships with them. There's a genuine joy in establishing meaningful connections whether they *lead* to something or not.

The number of networking activities you do depends on personal choice and need, how busy you are, and the results derived from the various activities. It's not a "one size fits all" situation, but highly variable among people and professions.

7

RAISING YOUR PROFILE

GETTING INVOLVED

Winston Churchill said, "We make a living by what we get. We make a life by what we give."

It's one thing to be a member of a trade organization or networking group. However, in order to take things to another level it's vital to get more involved in the group by seeking and accepting leadership positions. This automatically helps you to be perceived as more of a center of influence. Whether or not you're actually more valuable as a networking partner due to your position, you're usually perceived as being so. Leadership confers more credibility, power, and status within a group. When you have a visible leadership position, others notice you more and tend to have respect for you. Your profile within a group can be dramatically increased by a higher level of involvement and the acceptance of leadership roles.

You can volunteer to start a new chapter or group, to lead or facilitate a group, or even to do a presentation in front of a group. A lot of people join groups but then fail to participate in any meaningful way. They're often the ones who question the value of the group or complain that they aren't getting any referrals or leads. Get involved by volunteering or joining a committee. That will allow you to forge new relationships and deepen existing relationships. You can also be a GIVER and make a meaningful contribution to the group.

Involvement of any kind or degree raises your visibility in a given organization. People will know who you are and what you do, and will probably have a higher level of respect for you because of your proven involvement and leadership skills. The higher your profile and the better known you are, the more likely you'll get referrals and introductions that can increase your business.

As you're doing work in a leadership or committee position, do your best and try not to remain focused on the business you're getting. Other members will observe the quality of your work, and that might lead to some referrals. Show up to meetings on time, be consistent in your attendance and involvement, and be a team player. People who work with you will get to know you better and like you more, and you'll have positive outcomes. You're in essence presenting a kind of "work sample;" you're demonstrating your consistent punctuality, discipline, competence, and interpersonal skills. Don't be bossy, stubborn or egotistical. Be a team player! Networking can be a form of teamwork, especially when a number of people are all part of a single referral. For example, on a commercial relocation, a furniture dealer, a space planner, a commercial real estate broker, a technology specialist, and a commercial mover could all be members of the same networking or trade organization. They all might all be a part of a referral to the same client or end user. This team (a strategic alliance) will be together in meetings or conference calls, and are all part of the same team charged with successfully completing a commercial relocation.

Related to teamwork is one's commitment to a group. When a referral opportunity arises do you think of fellow members and make the effort to refer them? I notice that in every group there's a wide range in level of commitment, and that those who are more involved and more committed, and give more ultimately get more back in return. When you give referrals or advice do so generously and **without keeping score**. Trust that if you help others, give strong referrals, and get deeply involved, good things will come back to you in abundance.

Some people spend considerably more time and energy networking than others. The important factor is the quality of your networking time rather than the quantity of time spent. If you have a limited amount of time to spend networking, then it's critical to make the most of that time. The important thing is to be fully present at every meeting or event you attend.

Your degree of involvement and your relative position within a group can determine your perspective. When we're in a leadership position, it's likely to alter our perspective of the group. Other related factors are longevity and the level of allegiance to a group. Are we a leader or are we on the periphery? A good example is a class. My perspective of a class is quite different when I'm the teacher, versus being a student. When I'm teaching a class, I attend every session, and am in attendance from beginning to end, and the class can't start until I begin the lesson. I'm also more concerned about the outcome of a given class than my students. A sports team provides another good example. The captain, leader, or star of a team has a different perspective about the team than a reserve or the team manager. A more extreme example is the President of the United States, who certainly has a very different perspective on America than the average citizen.

The concept of giving is emphasized by virtually every author on the topic of networking. In their book *Power Networking,* Fisher and Vilas (2000) actually define networking as "making links from people we know to people they know, in an organized way, for a specific purpose, while remaining committed to doing our part, expecting nothing in return."

> ### "It is every man's obligation to put back into the world at least the equivalent of what he takes out of it."
> ### — Albert Einstein

> **One great way to get to the center of influence in a group is to get involved, stay active and actually become the center of influence.**

NETWORKING EXAMPLE: THE GROUP LEADER

Ron is an attorney who's an active member of the networking group ProVisors. He has been the group leader of a chapter for several years. As group leader he has become the true nucleus of his chapter. Everyone knows him, likes him, and knows exactly what he does. It's his central position that allows him to maximize his networking potential in that group. He has final say about who can join his chapter. He also chairs the meetings of the chapter's Executive Committee. By being active, visible, and a central figure in his chapter, Ron is able to derive substantial value from the activities of the group. In terms of personality, Ron is dynamic, extroverted, and charismatic. He's a dominant personality and a very strong and directive leader.

THE NEXUS CONCEPT AND SPHERES OF INFLUENCE

In every group there's a central, key person referred to as the *nexus* of the group. For example, a group of friends are all connected through John, the person who knows everyone in the group. As a result, he becomes the leader or center of the group. The others look to him to be the catalyst or motivator. Bob and Paul are part of "John's group," but would not usually have contact with each other without John's initiation. In other words, Bob and Paul are friends *through John*. In this group John is the nexus. Networking has a similar dynamic. There is generally one person whom everyone seems to know and like, and who has considerable influence in a group. If you're invited to a group by such a person with a very strong sphere of influence, it might be easier for you to establish relationships within that group.

Other important connections are *strategic alliances* and preexisting relationships that might have occurred from other contacts or networking. An example of preexisting relationships is siblings or couples who join groups or go to meetings together. It's a kind of a "strength in numbers" situation, and is part of the reason we choose to attend meetings and events with someone else rather than alone. As we form, build, and develop relationships we inevitably run into those people in other networking situations. Over time they become allies and even friends. These alliances lead us to feel more anchored and comfortable in an organization by producing a sense of teamwork and camaraderie.

As we spend more time in a group we might move closer to the center of the circle or the nexus. The more regularly we attend a group the easier it is to have influence and possibly power. When I started in one networking group I was one of forty other attendees. As time passed, I spoke before the group and was on the steering committee for the establishment of new chapters. In addition, I volunteered to be speaker chair of one chapter, facilitator for another, and greeter at another. All of this involvement allowed me to know more members, and to become a nexus and center of influence.

With increasing nexus positioning comes the potential for a wider sphere of influence. As we establish strategic alliances we become more bonded and loyal to the group. Another aspect is making yourself valuable by connecting or introducing people who might have potential value to one another. You can become a "gateway" to people and industries within your sphere of influence. People who take leadership positions enhance the value of the group for themselves. Sometimes there is more than one nexus in an organization or group.

In order to be successful within a group, it's important to establish a positive relationship with the nexus. Because the nexus usually has a wide sphere of influence, it's to your advantage to know and get along well with that person. It's even better to become the nexus of a group yourself to maximize your influence and receive the ensuing benefits.

Networking Tip - To get to the center of influence in a group you need to work hard and consistently, take leadership positions, and listen.

NETWORKING EXAMPLE: CHANGE OF NEXUS

There are times when the nexus of a group changes. Take the case of Mary. Mary was the original nexus among a group of friends, and had introduced a close friend to a couple of people. The four of them got together and socialized. After a couple of years, Mary moved away and was no longer the nexus or even in contact with the others. Her friend Bob became the new nexus and introduced another person to the others. This phenomenon happens when one person is more effective than someone else in staying in touch and nurturing a particular relationship. Remember that the nexus position is not necessarily permanent and can change with the development or deepening of particular relationships. This phenomenon sometimes occurs when marriages break up and certain in-laws stay in touch (after a change in nexus) and others don't stay connected.

NETWORKING EXAMPLE: DERRICK

Derrick is a business writer who was an active member of ProVisors for many years. By his own admission he joined reluctantly, not thinking it had any real value to him as a writer. Over time he befriended the managing director of the organization and got deeply involved in the newsletter committee. ProVisors provided some substantial referrals to him. The real value to Derrick was the dramatic increase in the sources of outbound referral sources which substantially improved his value to his own clients. He liked that he was constantly learning about various specialties that he didn't know about prior to his membership in ProVisors. He favored the combination of breadth ("spread the net wide") and depth ("be selective") approaches to networking. He felt he could have gotten even more referrals if he wasn't so busy doing the work from the referrals he received. In an interview with me, he encouraged others to be willing to outsource certain tasks so they had the time to network and not get bogged down or overwhelmed with projects not as meaningful as networking.

The first significant aspect of this example is that Derrick became close to the managing director, which shifted his perspective on the group. The second was his involvement on the newsletter committee, which not only increased his number of relationships but also gave him additional referral sources, both inbound and outbound. His position within the group dramatically shifted to his advantage due to both of these factors.

NETWORKING EXAMPLE: DONNA

Donna is in the building management field. She networks primarily through one large building management trade organization where she chairs the Charities Committee. She has chaired that committee for many years and is active in the organization, is generous with her time, and is well liked. As she works on the Charities Committee, she doesn't solicit referrals or talk much about her work. Additionally, she attends social functions and is a nexus. Through this specific, targeted networking, Donna has built a wide array of loyal friends and associates. Business flows naturally from this seemingly effortless networking program.

Donna's hard work and dedication to the Charities Committee are quite impressive. These qualities provide a *work sample* that demonstrates to others that she is a well organized, competent person. Most people are so impressed with her performance as committee chairperson they're willing to refer business to Donna. They build a relationship with her through contact on committee activities, and eventually find out more about her profession and are sometimes able to give her referrals.

> ## NETWORKING EXAMPLE: BETTY
>
> I first met Betty, a relocation consultant, at a trade networking function. Shortly after our meeting her company awarded a relocation contract to my company. We would see each other over the years at various networking events. Last year, a very large and prestigious project was out for bid. My company was fortunate enough to be the successful bidder, and I worked on the project closely with Betty for several months. Shortly after the project was completed one of my colleagues asked me to recommend a move consultant. Due to my successful experience with Betty, I heartily recommended her and she was awarded the contract. We have become friends and continue to refer each other business on a regular basis; we have developed a mutually beneficial relationship.
>
> Our working side by side on this large project was what forged our relationship. We had the opportunity, and time, to get to know and respect one another. We each realized the other person was competent and easy to work with. I like Betty, trust her and know that she's highly skilled. Though competence is the key factor, it also helps build the connection when there are positive feelings (liking) between the people.

The best rule of thumb is the following: Say what you're going to do, and when you're going to do it, and then do what you say you're going to do when you say you're going to do it. Do this on a consistent basis. Deliver more than you promise. It's tempting to be overly optimistic about when you'll get something done. Don't fall into the trap of overextending yourself. By not keeping your commitments and promises you weaken any trust that might have been developed.

PUBLIC SPEAKING

One of the best ways to raise your profile and get people to know and remember you is through public speaking. Many networking organizations and other groups need and seek speakers with areas of expertise. Seize any meaningful opportunities to speak in front of groups. Try to provide useful information rather than doing a sales pitch. Get to the front of the room, prepare your content, and present it with enthusiasm and passion. It's especially helpful to provide hand-outs and other useful "take aways" for your audience. You can start out speaking for free to get exposure and experience with your presentation. You can fine-tune your Power Point and practice tailoring your presentation for different audiences, room types, and length of presentation time. Be sure to include a reference to a phone number, e-mail, blog or web site so audience members can contact you.

Potential customers might perceive a relocation specialist in one light, and a professional speaker with a definite expertise in another. This was never more evident than with my relationships with legal administrators. Years ago, when I was developing my business with law firms, I would call on legal administrators in an attempt to develop business. Many of them would not return my phone calls. However, when I spoke to a large group as "Dr. William Saleebey, author of *Study Skills for Success,*" they not only perceived me differently, but one administrator approached me immediately after my presentation and agreed to hire me on the spot to perform the relocation of her firm. The power of public speaking is strong, and if you have the knowledge and inclination, I strongly recommend that you make presentations.

> **Effective speakers never complain about the amount of time they have for the presentation. They make the information fit the time allotted.**

CHAPTER

8

KEEPING IN TOUCH

LOOKING FORWARD AND BACKWARD TO BUILD YOUR PERSONAL NETWORK

As we go through our lives it's natural to develop new relationships, have new jobs, and live in different places. It's common to move forward and to leave old relationships behind. It's the rare person who keeps in touch with everyone they have ever known. Whether it's people we knew in our old neighborhood, at our elementary school, or at our first job, the common tendency is to move forward. Few of us do a good job of keeping in touch with people from our past. In fact, for many people it's just too much work. After we graduate from high school or college we may or may not be interested in reconnecting with our classmates via reunions. The same is true with jobs or anything else we have participated in. Ultimately, it's a matter of personal choice.

I enjoy reunions and usually attend them. I'm sixty-one years old, and have attended every high school reunion since graduating in 1966. I've also built and developed new relationships, both personal and business, with people I wasn't even close to in high school. I have nurtured relationships over the forty-three years since graduating. I make the effort, through asking questions, searching the Internet, or making a phone call to reconnect with people from my past. For me most of this effort is motivated by curiosity and the desire to reconnect with old friends.

As our business careers evolve there's the tendency to lose touch with people. I suggest you try to stay in touch with those who were once integral to your business or personal network. This could be done via a phone call, an e-mail, a holiday or birthday card, or other form of contact. Many people use ACT or Outlook to remind themselves to contact people. I recommend that you contact people who are proven referral sources more frequently than those who haven't given you any referrals for business.

Here are some reasons to maintain regular contact with the people you've done business with: Your contact person at a company may leave; if you haven't stayed in touch through this transition you might lose the account or your customers might lose your contact information or call one of your competitors to give them their business. Reach out even if it's been a while. On numerous occasions I've contacted an old customer, have had them tell me that they were happy to hear from me again, and the business relationship has been rekindled. This is why some people send holiday and birthday cards. It's another technique that will help people remember you. The more contacts you make with people the deeper the relationship and the more opportunities for referrals and introductions. This is simple reinforcement of conditioned responses. If we don't reinforce our connections, they will be extinguished.

As we go through our lives we meet many people, and every one of them is a possible connection and a part of our expanding personal and business network. When things slow down a bit, reach out, reach back, and reconnect with someone from your past. You might be surprised at the outcome. I've done this numerous times. It's increasingly possible with the modern search engines of the Internet. I often Google someone from my past, find them, and send them an e-mail. I've gotten responses from these investigations, and have found a number of people who were happy to hear from me.

> **Networking is the art of going forward and backward to build and sustain relationships.**

THE CRITICAL IMPORTANCE OF FOLLOW-UP

Effective business networking requires follow-up! Without it, most of your efforts will be squandered. It's vital to follow up with those you meet and want to do business with and to do so promptly and regularly. Keith Ferrazzi, in his book *Never Eat Alone,* has a chapter titled "Follow Up or Fail." He strongly asserts that follow-up is the key to success in any field. We can meet people, exchange business cards, like them, have a favorable impression of them, but if we don't follow up, the relationship will probably go nowhere.

Follow-up can take the form of an e-mail, an invitation to LinkedIn, a cup of coffee, a brief note or a phone call. However you do it, it is critical you follow up with people. Our memory is selective, and as we meet more and more people we tend to forget those who don't follow up with us.

For whatever reason, most people are not too strong or consistent in this skill, yet it's one of the keys to success in networking and getting referrals. You can't expect people to do business with you based on a single meeting or simply getting your business card.

It's essential that you have an enduring impact on the people you meet. Networking is not about one-time meetings that lead immediately to referrals, although that may happen in rare cases. Valuable relationships take time to develop. There have been numerous times when I needed to build a long-term relationship with a person before either of us gave referrals. This is especially true when you're meeting a large number of people. Building quality relationships takes time and often requires many meetings in a variety of settings. On the other hand, you don't want to get overexposed. As valuable as follow-up is, you should be mindful of not overdoing advertising material, self- promotion, and e-mail blasts. There's a fine line between good marketing and overexposure.

Follow-up is an art. You'll learn about the effectiveness of your specific follow-up activities from the results you get. Follow-up is not badgering or pressuring others. Rather it's a consistent presence that makes it easy and natural for others to remember and respond favorably to you. Follow-up is especially important after meeting someone for the first time. It's easy to forget someone if you only meet them once and never see them again. Those who follow up stand out and are remembered. We maintain relationships by repeated touches and continuous follow-up. It's not something you do once, but rather something that you do repeatedly and in different ways in order for it to be optimally effective. Stay in touch with people who are valuable to you.

> **Networking Tip - Don't write people off if they don't give you referrals right away. Get to know them and be patient. Give something first.**

GRATITUDE AND RESPONSIVENESS

When you get a referral, lead, or request it's important to thank the person who gave it to you. Make a phone call, send an e-mail, or make a public acknowledgment in a meeting. The expression should be immediate and heartfelt. Some people like to show gratitude by giving gifts such as a bottle of wine, a gift basket, or sports tickets. These are optional but common in some industries and regions. It's not the cost of the gift but the thoughtfulness behind it that's more enduring. For example, if you know someone loves Pinot Noir wine, get them a bottle of that instead of just any wine. If they told you they have a Schnauzer dog, a Schnauzer calendar is preferable to merely a dog calendar. The specificity is important; it shows you're really paying attention to the details of the conversations and relationships that you have with your fellow networkers.

In addition to thanking the source of the referral, it's critical to respond quickly and completely to the person or company referred to you. You want the source of the referral to look good by having referred you. Do an outstanding job on the work referred to you. There's no substitute for competence. Continue to provide value on every referral you receive.

Whenever possible reciprocate by giving a referral to these sources. Try to create a cycle, but don't keep score. Give more than you get. Be generous in your referring, and when appropriate be lavish in your praise of the person to whom you've referred business.

> **Gratitude is a key element of networking. Be sure to thank others promptly and properly for all referrals. Show genuine appreciation.**

E-MAIL "TOUCHES"

The other week I counted the number of e-mails I send every day, including weekends, related to business generation. It's almost always over twenty, and sometimes exceeds thirty per day, every day. Often these messages are brief and only take me a minute or less each. In fact, most of them are brief and to the point — a *"touch."* Periodically I'll write personal messages to all (or most) of the building managers or commercial real estate brokers on my list, who are my best referral sources. The messages will always be personalized and ask if there are any leases that have been signed, which might necessitate my moving services. If I send twenty of those (all to people I know) I'll always get at least a few responses, and sometimes a solid referral. This method of firing off the e-mails allows my name to be in front of a large number of people during the time when I'm not personally in front of them.

The main reason for doing this is that people tend to forget us if we don't stay in touch. Something or someone else may block out the memory of us. Remind people you're still in business and that you care about them. Stay connected constantly with some kind of touch.

An organization named Eloqui, which specializes in teaching people how to present themselves effectively, has a great approach to e-mail "touches." They send a brief and catchy newsletter out every Sunday morning (an off time for most businesses) that gives a useful tip and a new word with its definition. The timing is unique, and the information is helpful and entertaining.

Electronic newsletters are an excellent way to stay in touch with your contact list. In creating newsletters, it's important to present useful information in a concise format, and not to merely advertise your services. You can offer advice, touch on relevant topics, or provide updates about your profession or industry. The newsletters should have an "unsubscribe" or "opt out" function so the reader can discontinue if they want.

NETWORKING EXAMPLE: ANN

I first met Ann, a move consultant, when I submitted a proposal for a job I didn't get awarded. She wanted to use my company, and liked me, but the other company's bid was lower, and she didn't have a choice in the matter. She had an unsatisfactory experience with the other mover, and we stayed in touch. I liked her a lot, and would see her occasionally at trade networking events. At one point I told her I was going to Italy and wanted to learn the Italian language. She mentioned that her husband taught Italian. I hired him, and took Italian lessons from him in their home for a few months. After that, she was able to give me some business, and we stayed in touch, always in a positive and cordial way. Then she got awarded a substantial move management project and brought me in, hiring me as her mover. Since that time I've referred a few projects to her.

This relationship has always been positive and friendly, and I reach out to her on a regular basis and we have lunch. We refer business to each other regularly. At one point there was a lapse of several months in our communication, so I invited her to lunch so I could learn more about different aspects of her business, in order to help me provide her with more referrals. This immediately led to multiple new referrals for both of us. It pays to reach out and stay in touch.

CHAPTER

9

BUILDING A SOLID NETWORK

CRITICAL MASS: IT TAKES TIME TO BE FULLY CONNECTED

IT takes a long time to build a continual flow of referral business. You need to meet a lot of different people, build relationships over time, and nurture them in a variety of ways such as sharing meals, gifting, and socializing. Above all, you must always do an outstanding job on the referrals that you get. If all of these things are in operation, then you achieve critical mass. You have so many people singing your praises that your referral business will become a continual flow.

I must admit there are times when I don't feel like waking up early for a networking meeting or going out to an evening event. But almost every time I go I get something positive out of the effort and the ensuing experience. I make it a point to get something positive out of every networking opportunity. It doesn't have to be related to business.

You must be willing to "stay the course" in your networking, and not to expect immediate results. It often takes repeated contacts with people for them to be willing to work with you. Don't get impatient; keep making connections and developing them. It took me many years to develop a stream of referral business from loyal and satisfied clients. Sometimes it takes numerous and diverse "touches" before someone warms up to you. Successful networking is a long-term process. There will come a point in your business networking where you've made so many diverse contacts that your referral business will be constant.

THE HALO EFFECT: THE IMPORTANCE OF POSITIVE RELATIONSHIPS

It becomes easier to develop new relationships when you have developed a solid reputation and when people are "singing your praises." Good news travels fast, and when someone makes a positive impression, especially on key people within a group (the nexus or leader), it goes a long way in improving your position in a group. If the president of an organization meets and likes someone and tells others, then others often expect to like that new person. Certain people develop a reputation or "buzz," and the word about them spreads. When a large number of people all concur that a person is likable, then the liked person can enter new situations amid positive expectations.

Statements like "He's a great guy" and "She's a terrific person" tend to give us a positive predisposition toward someone. We usually see what we expect to see. When people tell me my company comes very highly recommended, then I might already have an advantage over my competitors in securing a contract. In short, the more people who like you, the more new people within a given circle will expect to like you. Your reputation precedes you. When people consistently hear good things about a person, they're more likely to think favorably about them and ultimately make referrals to them.

I've often observed that certain individuals get noticed, make a name for themselves, and frequently get their name mentioned in a positive context. These individuals stand out in the crowd and rise to the top of their profession It might be based on their competence or the quality of their work. They might have gotten the blessing of a leader in a group. Whatever the reason, they're in an enviable position; from there they're able to build on their positive reputation and continue to outshine their competitors.

NETWORKING EXAMPLE: HEIDI

Heidi is a building manager for a large high-rise building in Los Angeles. When I first met her, she worked for different company. Initially she didn't know me and merely informed me about the various building requirements. Over time she got to know me by name and would give me the names of tenants who were moving. We learned more about each other. I found out she took painting classes, was married with no children, we were the same age (within 3 months), and she had two sisters. She found out about my teaching and would always ask me about my classes. Gradually, as we got to know each other better, she would refer our company to tenants who were moving, with increasing enthusiasm. I began to bring her See's candy, gift baskets, and wine as a token of my appreciation. We developed a quasi-friendship, and every time I passed her building I would stop by just to say hello. This is one of the best examples I've experienced where I built a networking relationship over a long period of time through friendliness, good listening, good service (my company did a great job), and gifting.

Heidi appreciated my visits and gifts. It was the consistent, long-term visits to her office that cemented the relationship. I never asked her to be loyal or enthusiastic about referring my company to her tenants. But rather, I always greeted her with a smile and called her by name. If she was busy, the visits would be quite brief. If not, then we would chat about current events and what was going on in our lives. The important point in this example is that the relationship was built over a long period of time with many "touches" and a gradual development of the personal relationship alongside the business relationship. Give your business relationships time to grow, and don't be surprised if they move in unexpected directions.

10

ONLINE NETWORKING

SOCIAL NETWORKING

NOTHING is changing as rapidly and dramatically in relation to networking as social, or online forms of networking such as LinkedIn, Facebook, Twitter, and Plaxo. They have emerged and currently present us with opportunities to network with people in ways other than face-to-face or telephonic communication. These forms of networking are changing so fast that any comments made about them might be obsolete in less than six months. What we do know about what has become referred to as social media is that it can provide us opportunities to expand our virtual networks exponentially. With that growth come some words of caution, lest we think that randomly collecting hundreds or even thousands of "connections" is truly connecting with others. Just like traditional networking, online networking requires you to actively engage with others and develop your relationships in a real and meaningful way.

It should be noted that online networking must be accompanied by other forms of networking such as face-to-face and phone contacts. I refer to this combination of approaches as *holistic networking*. Online networking allows you to have a digital presence, a free online advertisement represented by your *Profile* and online statements. I recommend that you select a couple of sites (I focus on LinkedIn and Twitter for my own use) for business and a couple for fun (mine is Facebook). Remember that just because Facebook may be "fun" or what you consider as a non-business social network you can still use it to your advantage with your connections. I also suggest looking for online networking web sites that are specific to your industry. No matter what industry you are in you can find a network that caters to it simply by doing a Google search.

For any site you join, the most important things to do are to write a detailed profile, continually update it as changes occur, and invite as many people as you know to become your friend or connection (and accept appropriate invitations). In your profile include current and past jobs and your complete educational history so that people get a sense about you. By doing this, you're allowing others to find a way to connect with you. For example, if you went to UCLA (as I did) then others who went there might feel some sort of connection through shared alumni status. In short, the more information about yourself that you include in your online profiles the more opportunities you will have for others to find you and make a connection. This will assist you in establishing a large online social presence very quickly.

It is important to build as large a list of connections (contacts) as possible. Whenever someone accepts your invitation to join (or you accept theirs) peruse their profile and connections to learn more about them and determine if they know anyone who you already know or might want to meet. If you happen to know someone they know it can be an instant way to deepen your relationship with them, especially if your mutual friend is close to them. You'd be surprised how many friends you have in common with others that you don't even know about. This is especially true in industries and professions that have a small community. If you take the time to build your online profiles correctly you will amass a huge list of connections that you may have never spoken with otherwise.

My list has grown to over one thousand on LinkedIn in a couple of years, and people are now regularly asking me for introductions to my connections. You don't need to know someone well to add them as a connection. Write personal notes with your invitations so that others know exactly who you're and where they met you. The note can indicate something specific about the nature of your relationship with them. This little step can make all the difference in the world as it sets in motion the online relationship you have with that person. People like to know that you remember them and have gone out of your way to find them online. It makes them feel like they have made a memorable impression on you.

The question arises in networking whether to spend more time face-to-face or online. The exact blend is a personal choice, but do both.

There is an abundance of online networking opportunities. Some sites are more suited to business networking; others are geared more toward personal/family connections and fun. LinkedIn and Plaxo are examples of the former, and Facebook is a good example of the latter. There can be an overlap, and some people announce business information on Facebook. Pictures are useful on business sites, and are an integral part of Facebook. Uploading pictures of yourself can help people learn more about you and get to know you better. As the saying goes, "A picture is worth a thousand words." So don't be afraid to share photos of yourself. It is especially helpful to post photos of things you enjoy doing, such as travel or hobbies. For example, if you love sailing, and someone in your network is an avid sailor but you don't know it, imagine the conversation you may have with that person the next time they see you if they saw a photo of you sailing.

You can also increase your web presence by having your own web site and/or blog, which is far easier than you may think to set up (more on this later). Using a multi-pronged approach to your online networking is critical to creating and maintaining a vital visibility in cyberspace. Don't be afraid to explore any and all options that available to create, nurture, and build online relationships. The Internet is ever evolving, and web sites today are made so that even the least tech savvy people can navigate with relative ease.

In addition to writing a detailed and compelling profile, it is important to continue to update that profile regularly as any aspect of your situation changes. Many web sites such as Twitter and Facebook offer a chance to update your status so that you can give up to the minute announcements about what you are doing or working on. A related benefit is that when you change status, others in your network are notified, and it raises your profile (which is a good thing in networking). Use this feature regularly, but don't abuse it. It is much more to your advantage to talk about the current project you are working on rather than telling people what you had for lunch today. Updating your status informs people of what you are up to at that exact moment, so be sure to use this feature when you are working on something you want others to know about.

Many sites also give you the opportunity to ask and answer questions that are posed periodically by members of the various groups. Time is always a variable, and if you don't have a lot of spare time, this aspect of the process is optional. But if you do have the time and inclination to do so and if you are truly qualified to offer an answer to a question it is highly advisable to do so. This can only raise your profile within your own network, but can also yield new connections with people who you likely would have never met otherwise. Furthermore, once you provide a quality answer to a question you develop a perceived expert status within your community. This is invaluable and can generate contacts, leads, and referrals far easier than if you just an inactive member of the site.

Everyone will have a different focus and different purpose for networking online. For some it's a way to build a larger, though not necessarily intimate network. For others it might be an online database of addresses, phone numbers, birthdays, or other pertinent information. Online networking can also dramatically assist business development and marketing. I've used it primarily in that area, and though it was not immediately apparent, the results are quite remarkable. I can introduce people, gain introductions to decision makers, have many sources for outbound referrals, and continue to expand my network and usefulness to others. A large and viable network is not only valuable strategically, but it's inherently enjoyable for many of the people I've interviewed in the research for this book. The statement "You can't have too many friends" rings true.

The great thing about creating a large online network is that it doesn't require much time to maintain once it is properly developed. You can communicate with thousands of people simply by updating your profile, status, or answering a question. Posting a new photo can draw attention to your profile. This makes online networking efficient and rewarding.

The way you utilize social networks depends on a number of factors, especially the amount of free time you have. If you're in business development or recruiting, you might spend a substantial segment of time building and nurturing your online network. The site you spend most of your time may be a professional business site like LinkedIn. You may use it daily as a way to find people who are in your network through the people you know. The real beauty in sites liked LinkedIn is how you can meet people through the connections of your connections. You likely have only a few degrees of separation from nearly everyone in your industry, let alone the entire population of your city or town. It is with this concept in mind that you can use these sites to expand your online network in a way that best benefits your particular business.

If your job is extremely time consuming you might not spend as much time with online networking, but it is advised to at least set up a profile so others can find you. Online networking is not intended to replace face-to-face communication with others, but rather to enhance it. The key to success in this area is "cross-networking," or using a variety of in-person networking in conjunction with online networking. Either form by itself is not sufficient in today's marketplace.

It is safe to say that social media is here to stay. When consistently used in conjunction with other forms of networking such as mixers, one-on-one meetings and committees, social media can greatly enhance your ability to network effectively. Though it might seem like a time drain initially, online networking will save you time in the long run. It's important to continually add contacts, update your profile and professional activities, and communicate with your connections. If you want to expand your virtual and actual network exponentially, online networking is a wonderful tool to do so. For recent generations who have been raised with technology, this form of networking will remain a vital component of any networking strategy. For the rest of us, we have the option to learn it and derive its various benefits.

> **Social media by itself is NOT holistic networking! You have to meet others face-to-face and have a human dialogue with them. Listen/talk.**

WHAT IS LINKEDIN AND HOW SHOULD YOU USE IT?

In November of 2007 my son, who is Internet savvy, recommended that I join LinkedIn. I asked him why and he gave me a few compelling reasons: it was a great way to do passive networking, it was a free advertisement, I could expand my network, and it would be a fun way for a "reunion junkie" like myself to reconnect with old friends, acquaintances, business associates, neighbors, and classmates from my many years as a student. I WAS IN!!!

I started by writing a fairly detailed profile (which I've since expanded) and invited everyone in my e-mail address book. The acceptance of my invitations came fast and abundantly, and I was hooked!

What is LinkedIn? It's an online business network primarily for professionals. It's free to join, though you can upgrade to a premium account, which allows you to have more tools for finding and contacting people. It usually begins with someone inviting you to join, which had happened to me several times before my son pushed me to accept the invitation. You can also go directly to the site to join at linkedin.com. Once you sign up (which is really quite simple) you create a profile that should summarize your professional background, educational history, and accomplishments, as well as awards, professional organizations, and web sites. A strong profile allows you to be found by former and current clients, colleagues, classmates, and business partners. Your profile should be as detailed as possible in order to attract attention to it. It's essentially a free personal advertisement or resume posted online for everyone to see and review.

You can and should add more connections by inviting trusted contacts to join LinkedIn and be connected to you (and your network). Ultimately, your network (which you can increase regularly through additional invitations and acceptances of others' invitations) will consist of your connections and your connections' connections, which links you to thousands of people. You can add people by combing your rolodex, looking at collected business cards, or going through lists of e-mails of people you already know.

The real beauty of this particular network is that you're not limited to your preexisting contacts. You can and should connect with other professionals through your own contacts. Whenever someone new joins my network as a LinkedIn connection I peruse their profile for pertinent information and look at their connections to see who we know in common and to determine whether I'd like to connect or re-connect with them.

In addition to connecting with a potentially large number of people, having a large number of connections and an impressive or interesting profile gives you increased credibility. You can also post job descriptions, ask questions, and get and give recommendations on the LinkedIn web site. I've used the recommendation section (both giving and getting) to great advantage. It's easy to write one, and people who might not sit down to write a formal recommendation might be more apt to post one online. This recommendation then becomes part of your overall profile. Getting recommendations is a testimony to the quality of your work, character, and talents. LinkedIn is a very powerful tool offering you a free digital presence seen by potentially thousands of people.

Another important feature of LinkedIn is the groups you can join. There are groups related to specific industries and professions, alumni groups, networking groups, and trade organizations. This can help you not only define who you are by association, which can lead to additional connections. By joining groups with others who have similar interests, you will make beneficial contacts. Once you've joined a group, you can ask and answer various questions, which will raise your profile on the site. You can also start your own group which will instantly give you visibility and expert status within your industry and raises your online profile in a significant way.

It should be noted that this book is being written in 2009, and changes to the LinkedIn web site are likely to occur. The changes will undoubtedly further enhance your ability to make connections and develop relationships. As of this writing, I have over 1,100 connections.

WHAT IS TWITTER?

Twitter is perhaps the most talked-about recent development in social media. It's a micro-blogging platform that allows you to write short messages of no more than 140 characters. These messages are posted immediately on the Twitter site for your network of friends (called *followers*) to see. Twitter can assist you by developing a following of other twitter users, which helps to raise your online profile. In your postings, you can give advice, raise pertinent questions, or give links to valuable information. It's quite easy to set up an account. Be sure to include a picture that's engaging, a descriptive and memorable bio about yourself, and a user name that's amenable to branding. Be sure to include a link to your blog or web site in your bio. This will help drive traffic to your web site or blog. You should follow people in your professional field who have a lot of followers, and follow the people they're following. You can go to search.twitter.com and enter keywords to find people who have similar business interests as you. The most important principles are: write useful content, share the content of others, and follow people. Your goal is to get as many followers as possible. It is quite simple to follow others: just find the icon that says follow and click on it next to the person you want to follow.

Here are some examples of my recent tweets (140 characters or less) posted at twitter.com/drbillsaleebey:

Networking success is enhanced by standing out and making yourself memorable in a positive way. It's not who you know but who knows you.

Building deep relationships and truly connecting to generate referral business is highly preferable to merely exchanging leads with others.

Holistic networking considers networking as a way of life that combines social media with the best of all networking, meeting face-to-face.

I will be speaking about basic networking skills to the Studio City Chamber of Commerce on October 2 at the Daily Grill.

Great social media tips from Chris Brogan. RT @chrisbrogan The Building Blocks of Social Media for Business http://chrisbrogan.com

Relocation of Law Firms - I will be doing a podcast tomorrow, August 25 at 3 p.m. on The Law Biz Forum with Ed Poll about moving law firms.

Radio interview this morning, 6/11 at 7 a.m. on www.voiceamerica.com**. NETWORKING POWER IN THE PHYSICAL AND VIRTUAL WORLDS.**

Some people are fighting the entire Social Media idea. Were they the same people who resisted the answer machine, the pager and e-mail?

BLOGGING

Blogging has become an indispensable tool for those who want to use the Internet to raise their online profile. The term *blog* is short for *weblog*, but in reality it's just a web site. Blogs tend to rank very well in search engines because they're always adding new content. Your blog should be considered your "home base." In other words, think of it as sharing a window into your world with anyone who visits your site. When you invite someone to visit your blog it is like you are inviting them to come over to your home. Just like in real life, you want your home to be presentable. Make sure your blog is visually appealing and easy to navigate. It shouldn't be cluttered with unnecessary or inappropriate content. It should have as much information as possible about you and what you do. An "About Me" section is a must, but you should also include photos, videos, and as much written content as possible. You can write articles on your blog that confirm you to be an expert in your field. Your posts should contain *keywords* that are appropriate for your business or field of expertise. For example, some keywords I would use for this section, were it to be on a blog, are: blogging, social media, blog, blog entries, and blog posts. This will help your blog to be recognized by search engine *spiders* (also called *web crawlers)* and raise your name recognition on Google and other search engines. It is critical to write posts on a regular basis, always paying attention to the keywords you use. The more content you provide for the spiders to find the more likely you are to have people visit your site. There are many blog platforms available, but I highly recommend Wordpress. It's relatively easy to set up and customize for your particular needs and goals. Wordpress is far and away the best blogging platform, and is used by thousands of professional bloggers. It is user friendly and easy to set up. It is beyond the scope of this book to guide you through the process of setting up a blog. However, you can do a Google search to find a simple tutorial for Wordpress. You should use your own web site name or URL (Uniform Resource Locator) when setting up your blog and NOT one that would include wordpress.com with the web address.

You will need to register your blog by purchasing a domain (web site name), finding a web host, and installing the Wordpress software. All of this is fairly simple to do, especially with the expert guidance of your hosting provider. I recommend using GoDaddy.com to buy your domain and HostGator.com for your host. You have many options for customizing the look and feel of your blog. With some effort and creativity you will have a functional blog. All of the other social media sites you are a member of can then drive traffic to your blog (your online home) via links, which will provide much information about you. Remember to include your contact details on your site as well as links to all your social profiles so people can find you online.

OTHER SOCIAL MEDIA SITES

There has been a proliferation of social media sites, and many people wonder which ones to join, if any. Plaxo is useful as an online rolodex and for posting updates on your activities. Facebook, started by a Harvard student named Mark Zuckerberg, to keep track of his friends, has exploded and expanded into older and younger demographic groups. I use Facebook more for fun and personal use than for business. It's important to use good judgment with what you post on Facebook or any site for that matter. Don't post anything you don't feel comfortable having everyone see. While you have options for privacy settings on virtually all social media sites you never know what might get out that could cause a problem. Don't do or say anything that could jeopardize the fine reputation you have so carefully developed.

There are many industry-specific networking sites and sites that are geographically- specific (just do a Google search to find ones appropriate to your field or region). Think of each site you join as a new place to post your business card or resume. It's beyond the scope of this book to go into every possible way you can increase your network online, but below is a list of many social media sites you should peruse and consider for your own use:

Professional/Business Networking Sites

- **LinkedIn** — The most popular networking site for professionals that allows you to connect with business associates, alumni, and other professionals.
- **Plaxo** — Plaxo allows you to organize your contacts and stay updated with feeds from many online sources.
- **Xing** — Business network that powers relationships for the world's business professionals.
- **Ecademy** — Connects business people.

- **MEETin.org** — Allows you to organize events in various sites so that you can meet face-to-face.
- **Care2** — Networking community catering to professionals who "Care2 make a difference." This site is ideal for green or eco-friendly businesses.
- **Focus** — Business professionals can help each other with their purchase and other business decisions by accessing research and peer expertise.

Social Networking Sites

- **Facebook** — The premiere social network on the Internet that has revolutionized the way people communicate. This site is hugely popular at this time (2009).
- **MySpace** — This site still has value despite being over taken by Facebook as the most popular social network on the Internet. Its advantage is the ability to customize your profile's look and feel to create a virtual web page any way you desire.
- **Twitter** — A social networking and micro-blogging service that allows you answer the question, "What are you doing?" by sending short text messages, limited to 140 characters in length, called *tweets*, to your friends, or *followers*.
- **Gather** — Networking community that brings people together around the things they love to do and want to talk about.
- **Ning** — This site actually allows you to create you own social network. If you feel inspired to do so, you can bring together business contacts, vendors, customers, and coworkers in a network you set up.
- **Tribe** — Users can search for favorite restaurants, events, clubs, and more in various cities.
- **Ziggs.com** — One-stop source for building your online brand, marketing yourself on the web, and simplifying communications with people.

Social-Media/Social-Bookmarking Sites

- **YouTube** — This is the most popular video-sharing site on the Internet.

- **Reddit** — Submit stories and articles on Reddit to drive traffic to your site or blog.
- **Digg** — Users can submit and browse articles in categories like technology, business, entertainment, sports, and more.
- **Del.icio.us** — Social bookmarking site where users can organize and publicize interesting items through tagging and networking.
- **StumbleOn** — Connect with friends and share your web discoveries.
- **Technorati** — This is a network of blogs and writers that lists top stories in various categories. You should register your blog on this site.
- **Squidoo** — Allows you to create pages about anything. Here you can give tips, industry secrets, and other information aimed to help other members.

Other Social Media Sites

- **Wikipedia.org** — User-generated encyclopedia, where you can create your own business reference page.
- **43 Things** — Goal-setting site where you can gain a following of customers, investors, and promoters.
- **Yahoo! Answers** — Q&A service by Yahoo, where users can search for questions or answers in your particular areas of expertise.
- **Friend Feed** — Enables you to discover and discuss the interesting stuff your friends find on the web.
- **Ustream** — Streaming video site where you can host your own Internet TV show.
- **Flickr** — Outstanding image-sharing site.
- **WikiHow** — Raise your profile by adding tutorials and guidCreate a how-to guide or tutorial on wikiHow to share a small sample of your company's services with the public for free.

SOCIAL MEDIA NETWORKING TIPS: A RECAP

Social networking allows you to increase your online or digital presence, creating a free advertisement for yourself to promote your business. When starting out, I recommend that you select two or three sites to build your social network, and explore others if time allows. Personally I place most emphasis on LinkedIn, Twitter, and Plaxo for my business-oriented social networking, and

Facebook for friends and family (but also include selected business contacts). The most important aspects of social networking are as follows:

- Make your profiles as detailed as possible, including your education, credentials, and employment history — any of those categories can attract people to your social networking profile.
- Invite or follow everyone with whom you've a business or personal relationship and accept invitations from others you know.
- Ask and answer questions to raise your social networking profile; it helps to join selected groups related to your interests and expertise.
- Peruse the connections of your network to determine if there are any potential networking sources.
- Take the time to acknowledge birthdays or the accomplishments of people within your social networking circle.
- Learn about people within your network to enhance conversation and deepen relationships.

Social networking is not designed to replace face-to-face networking, but rather to enhance it. It's available twenty-four hours a day, seven days a week. Additionally, by adding people to your social network, you can enhance existing relationships.

Having a large and vital online social network gives you more credibility and makes people want to get to know you. Social networking enhances your ability to make meaningful and valuable connections that you may have never made in an offline environment. Most importantly, it allows you to maintain and deepen relationships you have made throughout your life.

11

HOLISTIC NETWORKING

CROSS-NETWORKING

A highly effective networking strategy involves being in multiple groups, or cross-networking. In my case the two major groups I'm involved in are ProVisors and Bruin Professionals. I know numerous people who are members of both groups. Additionally, I'm frequently a guest at various chapters of both organizations. This allows me to feel more comfortable due to fact that I know more people, and to become more of a center of influence in both groups. The more you're out there networking in a variety of groups the more likely you are to meet old friends and people you already know. In addition, you might have a certain status or position in one group that allows you to network more effectively in another. For example, you could be Membership Chairperson in Rotary and a Speaker Chair in another group, and those positions confer more credibility for you overall.

Another great example of cross-networking is found on the Internet, especially sites like LinkedIn and Plaxo. These sites provide us with a digital presence, an online profile, and as many "connections" as we choose to include in our network. Over time, people see us *everywhere,* and our network has value in and of itself.

If you're active in various organizations, groups, neighborhood organizations, church, politics, and your community, you're cross-networking. By doing this you'll feel more a part of and comfortable in these various groups. Networking becomes fun and easy. It's recommended that your networking be diverse; the more sources of connections the better. However, you must be prudent in managing your time so that networking doesn't become a "time drain."

Holistic networking involves using every possible source to build and maintain your network. For example, it is advisable to be involved in both face-to-face networking AND social media; use breadth and depth; develop a quantity and quality of relationship; and to gain an understanding of the psychology and sociology related to human interactions. Holistic networking takes a broad view of the networking process.

> **Holistic networking! A confluence of sources like face-to-face, social media, different groups, networking as a way of life.**

NETWORKING EXAMPLE: RAY

This case is an interesting blend of cross-networking, unexpected commonalities, and "six degrees of separation." I first met Ray when I was doing a move referred to me by Craig, an ex-student of mine. Craig and Ray worked together. At a later date, I ended up handling a major project, and Ray was also involved with that new company. Ray and I had lunch, and I mentioned that my parents lived in a town called LaVerne, California. Ray told me his aunt also lived in LaVerne. Ever curious, I inquired where she lived. He said she lived in a mobile home park on Fruit Street. That was where my parents lived. I asked her name, and he told me it was Marjorie Birnie. Coincidentally, Mrs. Birnie was my Mom's best friend. This coincidence struck Ray and me in the same way. We continued to talk and found out we shared other things like humor and Middle Eastern food. Over time we developed what has become a long-term friendship. We continue to share business referrals to this day. It was that serendipitous relationship between his aunt and my mom that cemented the relationship, though we also had business-related connections.

Ray gave me an opportunity to secure the business at his new company, but there was a preexisting relationship with another mover that prevented this from happening. However, we share a hearty appreciation of voice impersonations, and continue to get together for lunch or dinner occasionally. The relationship went from primarily business to friendship. I'm confident that because of the close personal relationship we have developed, business will return to the equation.

NETWORKING EXAMPLE: BOB

This case is a great example of cross-networking and reaching out to assist in different ways. I went to high school with Bob. We were not close friends but knew each other's names and had a cordial relationship. In the course of my moving career he had given numerous referrals to my company in his position as an interior designer. I invited him to lunch as a way of thanking him and cultivating new referrals, and he mentioned he was unhappy with the firm where he was employed. I had previously been networking with another designer/architect who mentioned he was looking for a new designer. I told Bob, who called the designer and was hired. This took initiative on my part to make the connection, but it had very positive consequences in my relationship with both Bob and the designer.

I like helping people and putting people together through introductions. I don't do it for what I can gain, but rather for the inherent satisfaction of furthering someone else's career and improving their life. A by-product of this approach is that people often remember being helped and supported, and eventually return the favor.

12

WIDEN YOUR NETWORK

SIGNIFICANT OTHERS AND FAMILY NETWORKS

WE can expand our own network significantly through our significant other, spouse, friends, family, and their networks. Networking organizations often invite partners to social events. I've experienced strong and positive connections with partners of members. The more open and socially versatile we are, the better chance we have of making more positive connections.

Something happened to me that had a huge impact on my thinking and perceptions, not for potential business, but because it proved once again that *you never know*. I was at my nephew's home visiting with him and his family when I noticed a picture on his table. The man in the picture looked familiar, strongly resembling a person named Rick in my networking group. I did a double take, and asked my nephew the person's name. My nephew Steve confirmed my suspicion that the person in the picture was indeed the same person in my networking group, and we both remarked how coincidental this was. Rick had actually attended my sister's memorial service prior to our being introduced. This event is significant in several ways. First, it proves once again you never know how you might be connected to others. Second, it reinforces the importance of maintaining positive relationships. Finally, it lends more credence to the "six degrees of separation" concept.

Another example is our children's networks, especially the parents of our children's friends. We might find out one of our child's friend's parent is someone we want to meet. It's important to be patient in this type of situation. You should get to know the parent on a social level first, and when the time is right, after you've developed some type of relationship, then you might shift the discussion to business. Every situation is different and you need to be sensitive to peoples' privacy.

DIFFERENT TYPES OF RELATIONSHIPS

We all have close friendships and family relationships. Often we want to help those closest to us. We treat this "inner circle" differently than we might treat business relationships. This is only natural. We're more likely to go out of our way to help dear friends and loving family members than strangers. This could take the form of passing along business, referring others to them, or assisting them in getting a job or other position.

Another example is when a business associate or networking associate becomes a friend (or a relative). In this case, the relationship has shifted from a business relationship to a personal one. Usually this happens over time, and with the change comes increased loyalty and exchange of business referrals. I've observed this happening in my own networking groups. We can't expect everyone with whom we do business to become a friend. But it's a positive development when we have cultivated a relationship to that degree.

I'm a proponent of developing relationships and allowing them to become social and personal if it's mutually agreed on. This could take the form of having dinner as couples, socializing, and even taking joint vacations. Of course this is a personal choice, and not everyone wants to mix business with their social lives.

My own family provides an interesting example of how we sometimes keep personal relationships separate from business. Every two years my father's family has a reunion in San Diego, California, attended by about 60+ people from around the United States. During the reunion we don't usually focus on business or business networking. In fact, many of us don't know much about what the others do for work. We focus on our family connections, and business is secondary or ignored. I've wondered what would happen if everyone put their business card into a pile, have them copied, and for those interested, to see if there's any opportunity for business synergy. It's a matter of personal choice about the degree to which we mix personal/family relationships with business.

MY PERSONAL NETWORKING PROGRAM

As Regional Manager, Corporate Relocations, in sales and business development for a large and well established commercial relocation organization, it's my job to find potential sources of commercial relocation business, sell my services, and manage and coordinate relocation projects. There are times when I spend as much as 50 percent or more of my time doing business networking, so my regimen is probably more rigorous and intense than most people. I'm active in both ProVisors and Bruin Professionals. I attend my chapter meetings in both groups, and also attend frequently as a guest of various regional chapters. In an average month, I attend 4 to 5 ProVisors meetings and 4 Bruin Professionals meetings. In addition, there's one follow-up troika or mini for each of those meetings. Consequently, in an average month I attend a total of about sixteen morning or lunch networking meetings. I also attend two "affinity groups," in addition to regular ProVisor meetings, in the Entertainment and Real Estate areas.

To increase my presence further, I usually attend a weekly evening networking mixer for either ProVisors, BP (these are both "general networking organizations"), Building Owners and Managers Association, International Facility Management Association, or some other specific trade organization. All told this is an intense networking schedule. I'm meeting new people constantly and reconnecting with people I already know.

The above describes the majority of my face-to-face networking activities. Lately I'm also doing presentations and seminars on business networking, which raises my profile within all of the groups in which I am a member. I also spend 10-15 hours a week doing Internet networking, primarily through LinkedIn, Twitter, Facebook and Plaxo. The primary activities are: inviting others into my network and accepting others' invitations to join theirs, seeking and providing recommendations, and perusing the contacts of others in my network. Through these processes I can make and seek introductions. My digital profile is rapidly expanding and my name appears increasingly on Google and other search engines. There's a positive interplay between the in-person networking and online activities, which is an example of holistic networking.

The result of all of these efforts is the massive number of direct business referrals I receive. I'm also able to make numerous referrals to lawyers, accountants, consultants, real estate brokers, and others. As I said, my networking program is more extensive and intense than most people. One reason is the nature of my business, commercial relocation. I need and thrive on referrals, and few if any of my competitors network in these circles. Therefore, I have almost no direct competition in this networking framework. Another reason for my passion and enjoyment for networking is my natural gregariousness and love of people. I enjoy meeting people and nurturing new relationships. I have a genuine curiosity about people, both the ones I currently meet and the ones I've known at various points in my life. In fact, part of my passion for online networking is directly related to this curiosity.

I have control over my schedule so I can book a large number of networking events in a given week and attend them all. Since most people don't have as much time, interest, inclination or stamina to network as intensely as I do, I'll discuss some alternative styles and emphases.

NETWORKING EXAMPLE: STAN

Stan does the same type of work as I do, selling and coordinating commercial relocations. His networking focus is very specific: he networks primarily with *commercial real estate brokers*. He meets them, keeps a detailed data base of his numerous contacts, and has frequent contact with the brokers he knows.

In addition to meeting and nurturing the brokers, he asks for leads and referrals and gets many. He also emphasizes giving gifts (often bottles of wine and restaurant gift certificates), and he likes to socialize with the brokers. He plays golf and attends social events with them on a regular basis. This targeted approach has been extremely beneficial to his business development efforts. He eschews the "open networking" I do and prefers to focus specifically on the commercial brokers.

This approach is focused, specific, and successful. Stan spends his time, efforts, and money on commercial brokers because he considers them to be his most suitable referral source.

NETWORKING EXAMPLE: MICHELLE

Michelle is a full-time legal administrator with a large national law firm. Her networking is done exclusively with an organization called Association of Legal Administrators (ALA). She attends monthly meetings, serves on the Membership Committee, and usually attends the national conference which is held at different locations throughout the United States. Her networking is not designed for business development, but rather allows her to remain current in her field and build relationships, not only with her fellow legal administrators, but also with vendors who attend ALA events and conferences. It should be noted that vendors (salespeople who are not legal administrators) who attend trade organization events should be sensitive to the fact that most attendees are interested in interacting with fellow administrators; they are not interested in being solicited for business by vendors.

By staying involved with professional colleagues through a consistent involvement with ALA (both locally and nationally), Michelle has numerous contacts that she could leverage if she ever needed to find work. In his book *Dig Your Well before You're Thirsty* (1990), Harvey Mackay recommends we network on a consistent basis over time and not just when we're looking for business or a job.

NETWORKING EXAMPLE: KIM

Kim does public relations work for small businesses. When I met her in a small group setting she had her brochure and portfolio and began the session by showing them to us. It was clear she needed immediate business from fellow networkers. This isn't inherently bad, but it is preferable if people don't appear desperate for business. One of the ways various members in networking groups differ is the degree to which they need business. If we appear too needy or desperate it doesn't present a good image to others.

Even if you do *need* the business, try not to be too obvious. Get to know people, show a genuine interest in them, and try to disguise any hint of desperation. If you appear desperate it may harm your chances of receiving leads or referrals because fellow networkers might conclude that for some reason you're unsuccessful or incompetent.

CHAPTER

13

DO'S AND DON'TS OF NETWORKING

STEREOTYPING

As human beings, we have a tendency to stereotype people who are different from us. If we encounter a youthful looking financial planner we may assume that he isn't experienced. Or if we meet someone who is over sixty, we might assume they don't listen to hip hop music. There are countless ways we might generalize and stereotype others: by profession, by accents, by physical appearance, by their name, by age, by ethnicity, by place of birth, or by how they dress. Alternately, we might assume we have something in common with someone because of a particular characteristic. For example, when you meet someone of your ethnic background, you might assume you have the possibility of a strong connection. But they may not embrace that characteristic or may not want to relate on that basis. When I find out someone is of Lebanese descent as I am, I might test out the connection on that basis. The larger the sub-group (i.e., men, women; Caucasians) the less likely we'll be to make a connection solely on that basis. For example, meeting someone who also went to college will not likely be the primary basis of connection. Having gone to the same school will narrow the sub-group. But the location of the encounter also plays a role. For instance, if I meet someone in Los Angeles who also went to

UCLA, the shared alumni status will not be as impactful as it would be if I met them in Africa.

With the variety of people I meet, the more I'm convinced of the dangers of stereotyping people. Granted, some people are much more likely to be good sources of business than others. But there are many surprises. I've met people I thought would be great referral sources and were not, and many whose value I doubted who turned out to be primary business partners. Once again, **you never know.**

As we get to know people better, stereotypes tend to decrease. We might prejudge or stereotype someone who's beautiful or handsome based primarily on their looks. As we get to know them, their physical appearance becomes less important and we focus on other characteristics like their intelligence or competence.

> **Networking is about connecting with others and finding various ways to assist and empower them. Don't assume too much or prejudge.**

POLITICAL AND SOCIAL CORRECTNESS

There are a number of topics present in human interaction not usually spoken about publicly. We notice some or all of these factors when we meet people but are often not able, and in many cases shouldn't, speak about them.

Following are some examples of such topics:

- Good looks/bad looks
- Age
- Ethnicity
- Accents
- Height
- Weight
- Politics
- Religion
- Personal Hygiene
- Food on the Face

- Body Odors
- Disliking Someone
- Embarrassing/Awkward Moments
- Incompetence
- Finances
- Health/Illness
- Clothes/Attire
- Where We Live
- Life's Disappointments
- Divorce, Conflict

Any of the above topics may be discussed, but you need to use good judgment and discretion in doing so. The topics can be sensitive to some people and potentially polarizing. Some people are comfortable asking about another's ethnicity, while others are reticent to do so. Interestingly, the more controversial the topic the more potential it has for deepening a relationship. But the opposite can also be true, especially when we have a very different opinion or point of view from the other person with whom we're interacting. We might connect with one person because of similar political or religious views and alienate someone else who has a different point of view. Some of these factors have regional or cultural components. For example, asking about someone's ethnicity may be common in some regions and unacceptable in others. Whether we argue or try to remain agreeable will differ from situation to situation. Some people actually seek a contentious banter and like arguments, though this behavior has potential risks in networking.

We all have some preconceptions about the world, and can't or should not talk about all of them in a business setting. Furthermore, there's a huge difference among groups in terms of acceptable language and behavior. Some groups are formal and polite while others are raucous and raunchy. There are many variations in between those two extremes. What is perfectly acceptable in one situation might be unacceptable in another. Examples of this are certain types of humor and so-called dirty jokes.

You need to read each situation and determine appropriate conversation and behaviors. People with high emotional intelligence and good intuition usually know what is appropriate or inappropriate.

NETWORKING EXAMPLE:
I DON'T LIKE HIM BUT I NEED HIM

There are times when you meet someone and simply don't like, connect, or click with that person. What happens if that very person could really help you and provide referrals? This can present a real dilemma. At that point you could either look for other, similar referral sources, or "suck it up" and try to establish a connection. If you want to give it a shot, you might want to find out about the other person. Maybe they're an introvert, or there is some other reason why you couldn't connect with them. Perhaps they might have offended you by a comment they made. Another reason you might not make a connection is when someone is overly serious or "all business." You might just need some time, or to try a different angle like talking about something else they are interested in. Don't let your first impressions become binding; be willing to alter them with new information.

I met a broker I didn't connect with initially because he didn't seem to have any interest in a business relationship. At one point he gave a presentation I liked, so I wrote him an e-mail in praise of his presentation in order to connect with him from a different angle. He responded immediately and indicated he would keep his eyes open for possible referrals. I'm certain that it was my compliments about his performance that turned the relationship around. Over time he has not only given me referrals, but also has introduced me to other people in his office who have given me referrals.

Remember that not everyone is like you or shares all of your values. We might have certain strongly held values such as the value of punctuality and formal clothing attire. When others don't share that value, we can either punish them or allow some leeway and "cut them some slack." You'll have a wider array of connections if you practice some tolerance and forgiveness when others don't meet your standards. Don't impose your values on others because we're all different in many ways.

Difficulty in connecting happens often when dealing with self-centered and narcissistic people. With these people it's "all about them." The best overall way to deal with a self-involved person is to ask them about themselves. They will typically be VERY happy to talk about themselves. Don't expect them to be interested in you, except as it might benefit them. From my own personal experience, this can be one of the most difficult types of people. In general, when you're dealing with difficult, stubborn, self-centered, critical, unfriendly, or overly dominant people, DON'T TAKE IT PERSONALLY. Be creative in trying to make a connection or "click" with them. E-mail is a great way to network with people who are like this, as shown in the previous example. Conventional and usual methods of communication will probably not work with these types of people. Even though we may perceive someone in a negative light, be careful not to diagnose someone too quickly or with finality. They might be having a bad day or acting out of insecurity, not ego.

Remember that not everyone is like you or shares all of your values. We might have certain strongly held values such as the value of punctuality and formal clothing attire. When others don't share that value, we can either punish them or allow some leeway and "cut them some slack." You'll have a wider array of connections if you practice some tolerance and forgiveness when others don't meet your standards. Don't impose your values on others because we're all different in many ways.

NETWORKING EXAMPLE: THE AWKWARD LUNCH

The following is my account of a lunch "troika" with four people: we'll call them Tom, Fred, and Ken. The fourth was me. Tom is a stockbroker from New York. He began the meeting by stating strong opinions about recent films and politics (the 2008 Presidential election pitting Democratic nominee Barack Obama against the Republican nominee John McCain). I was immediately annoyed, primarily because all of his opinions were diametrically opposed to mine. So, I was polarized from Tom. After a brief foray into films and politics, Ken, not yet an official member of the networking organization took the leadership of the group and suggested we talk business. It turned out that he was a competitor of Fred's, and it was very clear from Fred's body language that he didn't like Ken or what he was saying. Ken confronted Fred about Fred's attitude, but Fred didn't respond to the comment or admit his dislikes or concerns about what Ken was saying. There was disharmony between Tom and me, and between Fred and Ken. The "vibes" were not good. It was not a productive or enjoyable lunch. I was relieved when lunch was done and we could all leave. The meeting was characterized by rancor rather than harmony or synergy. This example is uncommon and does not represent the positive aspects of business networking. Some situations like this are difficult to counter and improve. However, there are cases when you can redirect the conversation or change the subject for a different outcome. You could also physically move, go to the restroom, or simply change the subject to see if you can get unstuck. Smoothing the tensions and redirecting the discussion to amenable and fruitful topics might elevate your status within the group as a peacemaker.

So, while there are times when politeness and harmony prevail, there are other cases when people just don't get along with one another. They might have marked differences of opinion, different values, and different expectations. It could be a matter of an off-color joke, profanity, or a strongly stated opinion not shared by others, or personal agendas and conflicts.

WHEN NOT TO NETWORK

It should be noted that not all moments are opportune moments to network and pass out your business card or brochure. Timing is everything. Here are some examples of times and places where you should NOT network, at least not blatantly.

- At a youth baseball game when the other person's child is up to bat
- At a funeral — You'd be surprised!
- At a wedding as the vows are about to be taken — Some people have no class!
- At the scene of an accident
- At the doctor's office
- Right after someone tells you that they're getting divorced
- After a major national or international catastrophe
- When the other person's mouth is full of food
- When someone tells you they're having a very bad day/week/month
- When you're conducting business with someone and need to focus on that and not on developing new business
- When the other person is busy or preoccupied

Common sense should give us a clue that even though we're face-to-face with a fantastic potential source or prospect, it might not be the proper time to promote your business. Proper timing is important for you to get the positive response you are looking for.

> **Networking Tip - When you are in a purely social setting, don't sell your business, use a charm offensive and get people to like you first.**

You shouldn't network when you're in the midst of solving a problem with a client or when they're upset with you or your company. Timing is everything, and you'll learn to identify the ideal time and place for networking and business development. There are times to relax and refrain from overt networking and marketing.

In the above cases, it's usually acceptable to have conversation, but not to promote or talk about your business. If we pay attention to others and have basic emotional intelligence, we should be able to ascertain the appropriate times and places for business networking.

PART 3

REFERRALS & THE ART
OF NETWORKING
MAINTENANCE

14

JUST KEEP GIVING

LOYALTY AND OBLIGATION IN GIVING REFERRALS

THERE are many reasons why people exchange business and provide referrals. Sometimes we refer people out of a sense of loyalty or obligation. If our child starts a business or profession, we want to help them. Another example is when someone is in our alumni organization, networking group, church, or service club, and the exchange of commerce is encouraged. We might feel a conflict between referring to a friend or relative versus referring to someone else who might be more qualified or competent. There's no one correct answer or resolution to this dilemma. When we know a lot of people who are in similar professions, we must sometimes make a decision to choose one person over another.

We're likely to be more giving to people whom we know and like and in whom we have confidence. It's also likely that we'll give to people who have given something to us. In some cases we're driven more by loyalty than by belief in someone's competence. It could be our dry cleaner, tree trimmer, rug cleaner, plumber, or mover. Some businesses give such generous gifts we feel obligated to use their services, but that's not the best way to make buying decisions. True and enduring loyalty is built between people over time through shared experiences. Loyalty needs to be maintained by all parties. People induce loyalty in others by a variety of means: calling people by name, giving gifts, sharing meals, going on outings, and developing deeper friendships.

Some people are very specific and limited in their loyalties to institutions, organizations and people. For example, some people will only make business referrals to others who attended the same university or were in the same fraternity. Others might be loyal to one specific networking organization or chamber of commerce. In other cases there might be loyalty shown to a particular real estate broker or banker. Loyalty is a matter of personal choice. When a salesperson changes jobs, the customer could remain loyal to the original company, the salesperson, or the technician who actually performs the work.

For people who are "power networkers" and know huge numbers of people, these issues can become more complicated. I know numerous financial planners, lawyers, and bankers, to name just a few professionals. In order to grow my own business, all of these people have a potential value, yet I can't possibly refer to all of them equally. I do my best to remain loyal to people who have provided me with the most referrals and assistance, but it's not always that simple or easy. There are fewer dilemmas of this sort when we know only one person in each specialty. Ultimately, the most compelling reason to make a referral to a client resides solely in picking the vendor/provider who's best for the client and the most competent.

> **"When eating a fruit, think of the person who planted the tree."**
> **— Old Vietnamese saying**

In many ways networking is the opposite of traditional selling: low pressure, generous, genuine, and giving rather than merely receiving.

MAKING THE EFFORT TO REFER AND CONNECT PEOPLE

Effective networking involves many things. Of course it begins with the connection, the establishment of rapport, and a real relationship. Beyond that, you need to do things in order to become an effective networker and to reap the benefits of networking. Be a giver in as many ways as possible. Giving can take the form of a simple introduction. Another area of potential value is to go out of your way to respond to requests and needs. For example, if someone is looking for an estate attorney in Phoenix, and you know one, it's important that you take the time to make that referral. The more you give the more you'll get in return in the way of relationships and referrals. Sometimes giving a referral takes a "leap of faith" that the person to whom you're referring will do a great job. When you have a high level of confidence in someone then you should refer them enthusiastically.

> **Networking is taking genuine joy in helping others through an enthusiastic referral, a guided introduction or just being interested.**

How Many People Should You Refer?

There's some debate among people who make referrals about whether to refer one person or more than one person for a job assignment. It depends on several factors. If you feel strongly one person is the absolute best for the job then you should only give that name. In some cases people ask for several names because they want to get multiple bids for a particular project. Businesses such as banks are sometimes required by law to give multiple referrals rather than one.

Making referrals is not something you should do carelessly. In order to make beneficial referrals you need to get to know people. When I hear someone's name mentioned repeatedly for doing outstanding work, I refer them to others. It's a combination of their competence, your relationship with them, and the effort that it takes to make a strong referral. You may like someone a lot but not know anything about the quality of their work. If that is the case then it's probably advisable to learn more about their prior work results so that you feel comfortable making a referral. The reverse may be true as well where you've heard wonderful things about a person but haven't made a connection with them and consequently don't feel motivated to refer them.

One very useful technique is to try to match people whom we consider to be compatible. This could be done in terms of geography, business size, or other factors that might make an appropriate match. Our "antenna" should be up continually in order to make the best possible referral.

David Ackert, founder of The Ackert Advisory, has developed a system called the Profit Boomers Referral Log which quantifies the numerical values of both incoming and outgoing referrals. The goal of this form is to reach a certain level of both giving and receiving referrals and to assign a differential value to referrals as follows:

Introduction to a referral source	1 point
Referral to a small to average piece of business	2 points
Referral to a large piece of business	3 points

There's a target of achieving a minimum of 8 points of outgoing referrals per week.

BUILDING AND GAINING TRUST: GETTING PEOPLE TO OPEN UP AND SHARE INFORMATION AND RESOURCES

Effective networking relationships don't happen overnight. It takes time to develop rapport and gain the trust of others. The more interactions we have the better we get to know others more intimately and gradually begin to share information and referrals. It's important to be patient and not to ask for too much personal information prematurely. For some people the referrals come quickly and frequently. For most people there's a period of getting to know and trust one another. After we get a referral, if we follow up, respond, and perform an outstanding job, people are likely to refer more business to us enthusiastically. We have provided value on a consistent basis and established a stellar reputation.

Patience will bring rewards, and with experience we'll learn to recognize the right time and place to discuss referrals and the exchange of business. Don't feel a need to ask for referrals prematurely. Most people don't want to be rushed or sold too aggressively. But if they know you better, like you, and trust you, then they're usually more than willing to provide referrals or ideas. This is especially true within the framework of a networking organization. Always be sure to contact all parties to confirm their willingness to speak to one another. Don't commit someone else's time and resources without clearing it with them beforehand.

People differ widely in how soon they're willing to give referrals or share valuable information. Some are willing to do so quickly, while others need the relationship to be more fully developed. When should we try to leverage our relationships? By having open communication with others we'll often get a good idea of another's readiness to share their contacts or refer people to us. You should have a conversation with people to explain your preference about how they should provide you with a referral. For example, you might prefer they give your name and contact information to others. An alternative is for you to receive the contact information and to follow up via phone or e-mail. Some professions and individuals are not permitted to do outbound calling. Patience in these situations will be rewarding in the long term. Great and rewarding relationships, like Rome, are not built in a day. In any event, it's often the networking organization itself that can encourage and even require referrals for continued membership. Some organizations periodically purge members from the group who are not giving referrals or engaging in acceptable referral etiquette.

15

THE TRUSTED ADVISOR

PROVIDING ADVICE, IDEAS, AND INFORMATION

ANOTHER aspect of the networking process is being a trusted advisor. You might not be able to provide a direct business referral, but you can offer significant value by providing advice, counsel or any type of useful information. In my own networking I sometimes seek ways I can assist others that are not directly related to business referrals. I might provide useful information about education, gardening, or raising children. I can provide advice about my field of corporate relocation even in cases where my paid services are not being utilized. People often remember those occasions of generosity and will later reciprocate with referrals. As we build a variety of relationships, we need to think creatively about the various ways in which we can be of assistance to others. **The core of effective networking is to give generously to others while creating and adding value to them whenever we can**. This concept is extremely important to remember and to follow consistently.

Sometimes people come to us with questions or in need of advice or ideas. It's part of the networking process to be generous with advice to our fellow networkers. It should be remembered, however, that our services have value and in some cases we eventually need to "start the meter" and charge for our time and expertise.

Some people consistently offer unsolicited advice to others. They tell them what they should be doing, how they should do it, and when they should be doing it. There's a difference between providing advice that's requested and dispensing it unsolicited. I get annoyed with people who are always telling me what to do with my life and what I *should* be doing. Parents are often guilty of this, and often their children tune them out. Be careful not to take the "nagging parent" role with your fellow networkers.

The Trusted Advisor

Some networking groups emphasize the concept of "trusted advisor" or "business partner." In other words, they encourage members to provide valuable advice and professional expertise. This contrasts with the term vendor, which is a person who is only seeking business. Most people who are networking are seeking business, though they may approach the activity with different levels of need and experience.

NETWORKING EXAMPLE: OVERCHOICE

I've gotten multiple referrals (and very good ones) from three people who are all financial planners. I like them all, and they all continue to give me great and frequent referrals. My dilemma is one of overchoice: I'm not sure to whom I should refer because I don't really know who's the most qualified or competent among the three people. I've resolved this by referring along the lines of geography, personality or style fit. For example, I might refer a younger investor to someone who is less expensive or has offices in their place of residence.

Although there are advantages to knowing multiple people who are in the same profession and specialty, it's sometimes easier when our choices are limited. As mentioned, I'm the ONLY commercial mover in several of my networking groups, which increases my chances for receiving referrals. But there are multiple people who are personal injury attorneys, insurance brokers, financial planners, and bankers. When there's competition, people must differentiate themselves in order to attain referrals. What makes us unique? Why should people give referrals to us and not to someone else who does a similar thing?

A common example of a profession with numerous choices is financial planner or wealth advisor. In my two major networking groups, ProVisors and Bruin Professionals, there are numerous financial planners. They are fee-based and non fee-based, experienced and inexperienced, young and seasoned, and work for boutique firms and major wire houses. At times it's overwhelming and confusing to try to differentiate between them. I asked them how they differentiate themselves; here are some of the answers I've received:

- They stay in frequent contact with clients.
- They take a mathematical approach to investing.
- Their firm specializes in research.
- They don't outsource investment decisions.
- They have high investment minimums (implying stature).
- They give free financial planning seminars.
- They publish a newsletter.
- They work on a team (which implies more service capability).
- They don't (or do) sell products such as annuities.
- They work on an hourly basis.

It's easy to determine that we personally like one planner more than another. It's more difficult to single out who's the best planner in a given group. If you're unsure about someone's qualifications or skill level ask them specific questions about what they do. Interview them without making it feel like a cross-examination in a court room. Think of it as if you were hiring them yourself. This will help you gauge their competence and ability in their field.

COMPETITION OR COLLABORATION?

Sometimes we're in networking groups with others who do similar work and we're actually competitors. Many groups try to avoid this situation by having only one person in each specialization; other groups resolve this dilemma through differentiation. For example, when there are multiple insurance agents one might specialize in life insurance, another in key person insurance, and another in long term disability. Some professionals are fine with having so-called competitors in the same group and collaborate and refer business to one another. If someone has more business than they can handle they can refer people to their competitor. Hopefully, the favor will be returned at a later time. In any case, we need to pay attention to this factor and address any concerns or conflicts before they become problematic. It's useful to maintain positive relationships with our competitors for both inbound and outbound referrals. Our competitors might even refer business to us if they are too busy or don't have the same specialization.

There's substantial value in building positive relationships, even with those perceived as competitors. You never know when that connection might be useful or beneficial to either person. You may end up collaborating with someone you had previously considered a competitor. You might be brought together though synergy or specialized expertise. I've observed professionals such as lawyers who refer business to other lawyers with different specializations for cases they either can't or don't want to handle. It's a good rule of thumb to treat others with respect. If you don't have something positive to say about another person, don't say anything. A large number of relationships might not seem to have any inherent value. However, you never know when something will arise and a positive feeling will stand you in good stead. Don't burn your bridges even with people you dislike. What starts as an unpleasant or negative relationship can turn into a positive one. Don't dismiss people who don't *seem* to have immediate value for you. Sometime in the future you might want a relationship with them, and there's more of a chance that you will if you treated them kindly and respectfully.

A related example of competition is a sports rivalry. A classic sports rivalry in my town is UCLA vs. USC. As stated, I'm active in networking with a number of UCLA alumni groups. As strong as those relationships are, they don't preclude friendships and business relationships with USC alums. Why would I reduce the potential pool of local referrals by 50 percent because of sports competition? The answer is: I wouldn't, and I count USC alums as some of my best friends and referral sources.

STATUS AND POWER IN NETWORKING

I've observed a phenomenon in my own networking experiences that I refer to as elitism. This occurs when people reject and minimize others who don't seem to have the status, power, or "clout" to help them. In my own networking it works as follows: if you're an attorney, accountant, or other professional, then you might be perceived to have inherent value. If you have what seems like a lower status career, then some people assume you possess no potential value as a networker. While it's true that some people have more power to make business decisions it's a mistake to dismiss someone because of their career, age, or appearance. There's an obvious difference between a young, inexperienced person new to a business with a freshly minted business card and a highly successful, seasoned, and well connected trusted advisor. In his book *Never Eat Alone* (2005), Keith Ferrazzi pointedly eschews the term **networking**, precisely because of the common connotation of desperate glad handing business seekers passing out their business card to everyone in sight. Ferrazzi's approach emphasizes meeting high-level and high-profile people, and that is not everyone's goal. Some people just want to make a good living, not mingle with the rich and famous. In reality, you never know if a given individual can put you in touch with someone you want to meet. They may not have the status or career that immediately attracts you, but they may know someone who knows someone to whom you're trying to connect. It's impossible to know everyone who's connected in some way to another person.

There's a wide range of opinions about what constitutes a "trusted advisor" or a person worthy of belonging to an exclusive networking organization or group. On one end of the spectrum is the belief that only certain select professions and individuals are capable of providing quality referrals. At the other end is the "you never know" position, which favors the notion that anyone could potentially be a networking partner or referral source for another.

A great example of this is found in the social networking site of LinkedIn. A person's contacts/connections might include business associates, friends, family members, ex-classmates, members of their church, neighbors, or members of their significant other's network. My own online network consists of well over a thousand people, and there's no way any business associate of mine could already know all of those people.

The real point here bears repeating: YOU NEVER KNOW! So, be careful with your assumptions as you continue to build your own network. This is not only fun and interesting, but it makes you valuable to others. I constantly meet people who are connected to others I know, and that fact alone can be the basis for a connection. When people realize how large and diversified your network is they'll want to stay in contact with you. Continue to build your network BEFORE you need to use it to get referrals or find employment.

The following example illustrates the importance of testimonials in establishing status and power within an organization. It's one thing to have Mom say how great her son is, but another when the managing director or president of an organization highly praises or recommends you. The plaudits from people in power have more impact, and should be sought when appropriate.

NETWORKING EXAMPLE: CENTER OF INFLUENCE

Greg is the Executive Director of a large networking group of which I'm an active member. Although I've met Greg a few times, we don't know each other well. He was attending a networking meeting where I was a guest from another chapter, and he noticed I was there and remembered that I had successfully moved his office. As we were doing our "needs, deals, wants, and testimonials," he spoke up and highly praised me and my company's work. The significance of this praise was heightened based on his position and status within the group. He spoke spontaneously, and I was thankful and know it has led to more business.

I followed up with a meeting with him and discussed the genesis and development of this book. He was interested and supportive, recommending several people within the organization for me to interview. I used his name when contacting these potential interviewees. That opened the door, and because of his position they were all responsive and helpful. Greg personifies the "*trusted advisor*." He's experienced, respected, knowledgeable, and well connected. His integrity and sphere of influence add weight to his suggestions and make his contributions more valuable.

NETWORKING EXAMPLE: S.M.

A few years ago a commercial real estate broker whom I didn't know called to ask me some questions about the pricing of relocations. She introduced herself and began asking questions. I answered them all despite the fact that I didn't know her. I took about 20 minutes and she thanked me for my time and information. It was a pleasant and cordial conversation. The following morning I ran into her at a networking meeting where she was a guest. As it turned out, she was so impressed with my helpful attitude that she has since referred me a number of projects. It was clear from her comments to me that our phone conversation had given her a favorable impression of me. Treat people well and they will reciprocate. You never know when basic kindness and the willingness to assist others will pay off for you.

PART 4

THE PSYCHOLOGY OF
NETWORKING

16

APPLIED PSYCHOLOGY

THERE are numerous psychological and sociological factors that influence networking. Some of them relate to us as individuals, some to group behavior, and some are a combination of the two. No single factor accounts for why we connect or don't connect with others. Motivation is a key factor. That is, how strongly are we driven to connect with certain people? Throughout this chapter you'll find a variety of factors that comprise the psychology of networking. As you read about them, ask yourself how much each of them influence your own experience with networking and other human interaction.

PERCEPTION OF SELF VS.
THE PERCEPTIONS OF OTHERS

We all have some type of self-perception. We might see ourselves as handsome or ugly, bright or average in intelligence, introverted or extroverted, agreeable or disagreeable, easy going or difficult. For some people, their self-perception is well developed. However, our self-perception might not match the perception that others have of us. You might say "I don't see myself as bossy, just organized." Others might perceive you as bossy. It's useful to know the various ways others perceive you, especially when those perceptions are negative in nature. It's also important to know if we have a positive impact on others. It can be informative to determine how closely others' perceptions of us match our own self-perceptions. For example, if we don't perceive ourself as a leader and others do perceive us as a leader, that can explain why they are always coming up to us with questions or problems to be solved. Another common example is when others consider us unapproachable, and we perceive ourselves as welcoming and approachable. In this case, our positive self-perception is negated by the feelings and perceptions of others. There's no objective truth in this situation; they are simply differing views of reality.

The concept of self-perception or *self-schema* refers to physical size and shape, intelligence, and every aspect of human personality. We might consider ourselves tenacious, while others perceive us as stubborn. Following are other examples of opposing perceptions:

- Confident or Arrogant
- Friendly or Glad Hander
- Determined or Pushy
- Funny or Silly
- Enthusiastic or Desperate
- Intense or Anxious
- Assertive or Aggressive
- Organized or Obsessive
- Responsible or Bossy
- Punctual or Overeager

It's unlikely anyone would describe themselves as a braggart, as arrogant or as a narcissist. One time I confronted a friend whom I perceived to be bragging excessively about his children. He got defensive, claimed that he was not bragging, just proud of his children. So what I perceived as bragging he considered pride. It's useful to ask trusted friends and associates how they perceive you, to be able to bridge the gap between self-perception and perception others have of you. For example, I don't perceive myself as defensive. However, if I'm accused of something I'm certain I don't do, I might actually become defensive or be perceived as defensive. There's a difference between clarifying one's feelings and being defensive. Often people are unable to recognize this distinction. This discrepancy can explain why certain types of interpersonal conflicts occur. In many cases we think we come across one way, yet others might be put off or annoyed by our demeanor or behavior. It doesn't mean we have to change, but merely to be aware of these discrepancies.

Related to this are the differences between our private feelings and perceptions and what we actually express to others. We might be acutely aware of our feelings or attitudes about others, yet they might be unable to detect them. For example, when we are uncomfortable with another's behavior, they might be oblivious to our discomfort. So, although we might find someone extremely annoying, they might be unaware of the subtleties of our feelings about them. In spite of this, we're often self conscious in social settings because we know our true feelings (even though others might not). There's a wide variation in terms of how accurately others perceive our true feelings about them. Some people can "read" our nonverbal communication and expressions which we might think we have disguised.

For example, when we don't like another person, we might demonstrate that dislike by turning away from them or averting our eyes. They may or may not perceive more subtle changes in body language. It's possible they might think you're just a cold person. Yet, as I mentioned, we might be successful in hiding our true feelings from others. This is especially true in a business setting where negative feelings are not always expressed openly. In some cases we might actually want others to be aware of our annoyance or dislike.

If you want to determine how others perceive you, ask several people whom you trust how they perceive you in order to validate your own self-perception. Different people probably have differing perceptions of you (your mom, your wife, your children, or your neighbor). You could role-play with a close friend or simply ask them what they perceive to be others' perception of you. In addition, continue to fine tune both your self perception and your perception of others as you change or gather new information. We can then utilize this new information to help us understand why people relate to us in certain ways and change our behavior that others might find offensive.

When we achieve certain results like success or failure, we often have our own theories or reasons about why things happened. For example, we might think we attained something due to our persistence, while others tell us we were simply the best-qualified candidate. In the 2008 United States Presidential election, President Obama was perceived variously as: calm, intelligent, charismatic, inspiring, and inexperienced. It would be interesting to find out why he thought he won the election. *Attribution theory* asks the question, "Why do we think a particular thing happens?" In other words, to what do we attribute the cause of a particular event? A religious person might believe something happened because they prayed for it or because it was God's will, while a non-religious person might attribute a result solely to hard work. A common problem related to attribution of cause called the *fundamental attribution error.* This refers to the common tendency of people to overemphasize personality-based explanations for behaviors observed in others while deemphasizing or not considering, situational explanations. In other words, people assume that others' actions are based more on what kind of person they are rather than social or environmental forces that might be influencing them. Is someone talkative because they're a "motor mouth" or because they're nervous at meeting their future wife's family for the first time? Be careful in judging others' behavior without considering the circumstances or context. Periodically check your perceptions to be sure you're considering all possible explanations for behavior.

> **Perception is important. There is how we see ourselves, how others see us, and reality which often lies somewhere in between.**

CASE STUDY — THE BILLY JOEL FACTOR

Looking like someone else, especially someone famous can lead to increased familiarity with others. People might actually project onto you their feelings for and perceptions of the famous person. In this subconscious process of identification, there's a positive transference or "connection by association." If this occurs, go with the flow and make them feel comfortable with their perception.

I've been told on told on numerous occasions (literally hundreds of times), dating back thirty years, that I bear a striking resemblance to the singer and "Piano Man" Billy Joel. We're roughly the same age, have the same body type and height, coloring, goatee, amount of hair, and eye shape. My sense is that most people regard Billy Joel positively, for his incredible body of work and charisma. Obviously I'm NOT him, but I look like him, and that has a positive association for most people. So, this likeness helps me. People come up and talk to me and have asked for my autograph. Others ask if I play the piano, which I actually do.

When people bring up the resemblance, I have an instant talking point, a way in to start or further the conversation.

This affects my networking in the following way: I'm frequently perceived as a kind of substitute for a celebrity others admire. Recently three people who were sitting behind me in an audience started a conversation with me asking if I was him. I said no, but it led to a positive conversation and some potential moving business. So when we look strongly like someone, it can mean acceptance (or rejection) by association because they're projecting their feelings about the celebrity onto you. It's worked in interesting and positive ways for me, so hopefully Billy Joel won't shave his goatee. This is another excellent example of the difference between self-perception (what I see when I look in the mirror) and the perception of others ("Has anyone ever told you that you look like Billy Joel?")

The significance of this factor is that people often make judgments based on associations. When something we do or how we look reminds others of someone else, they might actually substitute the "other person" for us. In this Billy Joel example, my resemblance to him is so striking that many people might subconsciously be relating to him instead of to me. Thankfully I resemble a person who's quite popular and revered by many.

The importance of this example is that people often transfer their feelings and perceptions of one person onto another. You might resemble a favorite brother, an ex-wife, or a deceased friend. The feelings for the substituted person might be positive or negative. In cases where the resemblance is striking, the effect is likely to be more pronounced. This example is based solely on a visual similarity between two people, which happens often in life. It can also occur when you act a certain way that reminds them of someone else. When we *remind* people of someone else, *especially someone famous*, it can have a significant effect on our interactions with others.

EGO STATES: PARENT, ADULT, AND CHILD

The late psychologist, Eric Berne, founder of Transactional Analysis, took Sigmund Freud's concept of *superego, ego*, and *id*, and applied them to modern people. He called these three main ego states: Parent, Adult, and Child.

The parent is often judgmental, telling others what they should do and when they should do it. The adult represents the normal business discussion mode. The child is more playful; we might exhibit this ego state with someone we know better and with whom we're able to "let our hair down" and have fun. There's likely to be laughter and even silliness in the child ego state. This concept is useful in understanding how we behave in our business lives. Are we serious and mature (adult), judgmental (parent), or more playful and spontaneous (child)?

Most business is conducted in the adult mode. The more interesting applications are the child and parent. Laughter is a strong representation of the child. Humor is a wonderful way to bond with others. A person whose conversation has a lot of advice and "shoulds" is probably heavily in the parent mode. "Parents" are often rule setters who like to set limits for the group and determine acceptable and unacceptable behavior. This relates to networking in several ways. The primary importance is to understand how the child and parent ego states influence relationships. Neither is positive or negative per se, but each affects our interpersonal transactions.

We're more likely to build deeper relationships by being willing to relate in the child ego state occasionally, and not always staying in the more serious, adult ego state. This is primarily evident in the use of humor and spontaneous, childlike expressiveness (both examples of the child state). The parent ego state, though sometimes perceived as judgmental, is also the state from which we operate when we provide valuable advice to a colleague or fellow networker. So, although we generally do business from the adult, the other ego states are also useful. None of the ego states are necessarily good or bad; they are simply useful determinants of human interaction. The important point is to pay attention to what you say and do and how others might be affected by your actions.

PERSONALITY TYPE: MYERS-BRIGGS TYPOLOGY

There are many ways to consider differences in personality type. One of the most useful and frequently used tools is the Myers-Briggs Type Indicator, which has been utilized by psychologists and corporations to differentiate people. According to this model personality can be broken up into four major dimensions:

Extroversion	Introversion
Sensing	Intuition
Thinking	Feeling
Judging	Perceiving

The extrovert-introvert dimension refers to the degree to which we are naturally outgoing and gregarious. The extrovert is more outgoing and sociable, and likes to be surrounded by others. The introvert tends to be shy, reserved, and socially reticent by nature. Introverts can also be deeply thoughtful or feeling, though they might not verbally express everything. Extroverts draw energy from being with others, while introverts may feel drained by being around too many people. Sometimes introversion or extroversion is situational. An extrovert might be reserved in a room full of strangers, while the introvert might be quite talkative at a gathering of immediate family.

The sensing-intuition factor focuses on whether we deal more with facts and personal experience or abstract concepts and ideas. Sensors tend to focus on facts, specifics, and their own experience, and are sequential, step by step information processors. Many accountants and lawyers are likely to be sensors. Intuitive people tend to focus on various possibilities, are more fanciful thinkers, and trust their instincts. Intuitive types are often involved in creative fields such as the visual, theatrical, or musical arts. In conversation, they often jump around from topic to topic and are imaginative and creative.

The thinking-feeling factor differentiates between logic (thinkers) and sensitivity/sympathy (feelers). Thinkers tend to value truth over tact, competition over cooperation, and logic over feelings. Thinkers are often competitive and motivated to win in games or contests. By contrast, feelers value tact, harmony, cooperation, and being appreciated. Feeling types tend to be sensitive and empathic to others' problems.

The judging-perceiving factor focuses on whether we are intentional (judger) or spontaneous (perceiver). Judgers like to make decisions quickly, prefer to make and keep plans, are well organized, and like to be in control. They tend to see things in black and white rather than shades of gray. At the other end are perceivers, who like to keep their options open, act spontaneously, are often disorganized, and are more casual and unconventional. Perceivers tend to be adaptable and comfortable to changing situations.

We're all a combination of the four dimensions, which may be referred to as EIFP (extrovert, intuitive, feeling, perceiving) or ISTJ (introvert, sensing, thinking, judging). The combinations can get fairly complex, but if understood in their relationship to each other, help explain how we go about our lives in unique and different manners. A scientist and an artist are likely to be at opposite ends of the thinking-feeling dimension. Similarly, a politician and a hermit would be at opposite ends of the extrovert-introvert spectrum. But despite wide differences in temperament and personality, there's still room for making connections. You don't have to be similar to someone in order to make a meaningful connection.

This model helps explain why some people click more than others. There's a huge range of differences among people. We tend to connect better with others who have a similar view of the world. However, it's useful to be versatile so we're not limited to relating to people like ourselves. For example, though you may not be an artistic person yourself, by being aware and versatile, you're able to relate to artistic types in addition to those more like yourself. I'm not a lawyer, but I've learned some of the ways that lawyers think and therefore can build a relationship with them. For example, I've learned that most lawyers tend to be logical and have an understanding and regard for empirical data. This understanding helps me in my communication with lawyers. If you're a Democrat, you're wise not to limit your relationships exclusively to other Democrats. The same is true of religious or other philosophical viewpoints. The key is to find a common ground with others, whether you're similar to them in Myers-Briggs typology or not.

The Myers-Briggs Typology and other such models of personality differences aren't meant to segregate different types of people. Rather, they can provide us with insights about individual differences and why we're able to connect more easily with some types of people than others. Extroverts are likely to thrive at large mixers, and introverts are usually more comfortable in smaller groups. The major keys to success in relation to this instrument are versatility and awareness of the dimensions of individual differences.

> **Networking Tip - If you're an extrovert, show up and do your thing. If you're an introvert, get the small group thing going.**

CIRCADIAN RHYTHMS: BODY CLOCK

Some people prefer to stay up late. They're referred to as "night owls." These people usually don't like to get up early. At the other end of the spectrum there are people who like to get up early, referred to as "early birds." Of course there are many variations in between these extremes. Some people even have their energy peak midday, and they might thrive at lunch meetings. Night owls are probably going to prefer and enjoy meetings that start later, and early birds will likely enjoy and thrive in early morning meetings.

My friend Bob and I have totally opposite circadian rhythms. I'm usually up around 5 a.m., take a noontime nap, and go to sleep prior to 10 p.m. He gets up around 10 a.m., does not nap, and goes to sleep around 2 a.m. He does not do well at early morning events (in fact he rarely attends them), and I have difficulty at late evening events. When we socialize at night, he's often just warming up by mid evening, at a time when I'm winding down. We can alter these natural rhythms by certain necessities, like when I teach a 6 to 10 p.m. class. I have to stay up until around midnight to unwind when I teach at night, and it takes me out of my normal routine, but I can do it.

I've observed "night owls" at early morning meetings, and they often look and act like zombies. They're not awake and at their best. Conversely, I've seen "early birds" fading out at evening events at 9 p.m., while the "night owls" are just getting warmed up. The key here is to schedule and attend events best suited to your personal body clock. In general, we tend to hang out with others who have similar circadian rhythms as us. My friend Bob would never take a 5 a.m. walk with me (he's still asleep at that time), and I wouldn't go to a 10 p.m. movie. We still connect and socialize, but have to compromise to find times that work for both of us. If you must attend events either too early or too late for your comfort, try to get more rest to compensate for possible discomfort or fatigue. Once you've determined your predominant body clock, you should try to attend events that are ideally suited to you.

ROLES AND THEIR LIMITS

We all play various roles in our lives: father, son, cousin, employee, committee member, golfer, shopper, teacher, or student. Sometimes our roles limit our ability to network freely. For example, if you're a preacher on Sunday and a salesman during the week, you won't preach to your customers or sell a product to your congregation. Some roles have strict boundaries about appropriate behavior. When I'm in the role of teacher I cannot actively solicit commercial relocation business. It's unprofessional, unethical, and against university policy. There are specific *boundaries* that discourage or absolutely prohibit these so-called *dual relationships*. We don't want our physician selling us mutual funds. When we pick up our dry cleaning, we don't want a political solicitation from our dry cleaner. We expect our professor to teach us, not to sign us up for a multi-level marketing scheme.

Sometimes we can have dual relationships that are socially and ethically acceptable. For example, it is acceptable to be both a parent and soccer coach for your child's team. We might be in the role of husband at our spouse's company party. It's probably better in that situation not to be too aggressive in our networking, or not to network at all. Common sense will usually provide us with cues and clues about appropriate behavior in those situations. What is important in this context is to understand the different roles we play throughout our lives and how they impact our various relationships.

Here are some examples of acceptable and unacceptable role-mixing:

Acceptable	To mention you play softball on weekends
Unacceptable	To sell Tupperware to your client if you're a lawyer
Acceptable	To mention where your child goes to school
Unacceptable	To ask a new client to baby-sit your child while you go to a party
Acceptable	To talk about a recent vacation to Thailand
Unacceptable	To ask a client if you can use their frequent flyer miles for your vacation travel

COGNITIVE DISSONANCE AND ITS IMPACT ON HUMAN INTERACTION

The psychologist Leon Festinger highlighted a fascinating aspect of human interaction which he labeled *cognitive dissonance.* The starting point is an attitude or belief that you have about a category of people. For example, let's say you have a negative attitude or prejudice about homosexuals. That represents your starting cognitive position. (You could substitute any group of people, like marijuana smokers, Swedes, or priests.) Assume you like someone named Bob who happens to be a homosexual. So you don't like homosexuals, but you like Bob. At some point Bob tells you he's gay. **At that point you're likely to get into a state of cognitive dissonance.** This simply means that there's dissonance, or conflict, between two cognitive states (you don't like homosexuals but you like Bob). You can either stay in the state of dissonance or change one of the two positions. That is, you either alter your position on homosexuals or you change your feelings about Bob. This is a common situation in human interaction. Sometimes our original positions or prejudices are so ingrained that we're unwilling to change them even in the face of strong evidence to the contrary. It's preferable to be flexible in our thinking and to allow new information to alter our biases and prejudices.

It's advantageous to be willing to change your original positions when you receive contrary information. It demonstrates flexible thinking and the willingness to change. More important, the ability to change both your thinking and your behavior widens your pool of possible connections. Inflexible, prejudicial thinking is limiting and not in your best interest. For effective networking, keep an open mind and widen your perspective.

17

GROUP DYNAMICS

GROUP SIZE

THERE can be a substantial difference in the dynamics of a group depending on its size. With a *dyad* (two people) there's usually the possibility of a more intimate exchange of ideas and information. In fact, quieter people favor this format in many cases. When a group expands from two to three, the dynamics are likely to change in some way. For example, you may have been having an intimate, confidential conversation when the third person arrives, and you then need to change the subject. You've probably experienced this when you're talking to someone one-on-one and a third person enters the conversation. When a group goes from three to four, the dynamics change yet again. In this case there are more possible variations. There could even be two separate conversations, or three people may engage in a conversation, leaving the fourth feeling left out. As the size of the group continues to increase, the discussion is likely to become less intimate or personal in nature. A dominant person might monopolize the conversation. One person might hold forth with stories, opinions or jokes, or otherwise dominate the discussion.

These phenomena are central to understanding how we make connections. Some people will only really connect one-on-one and avoid larger groups. They're "two's company, three's a crowd" people (exclusive), while others tend more toward "the more the merrier" (inclusive). We might be asked, "Do you mind if Joan joins us?" Your honest feeling is that Joan will change the tone of the group because she's a dominant personality tending toward telling the same stories over and over again. However, you might agree to have her join to keep things harmonious. Or you could state your honest feelings that you'd rather keep the group more intimate (and keep Joan out of the group).

In terms of your networking, it's quite useful to know which size groups are more conducive to establishing relationships. If you're an extrovert who loves large parties, you should seek those large festive events because they suit your style and personality. On the other hand, if you're more of an introvert you'll be better off one on one or in smaller groups. Ask yourself the question: In what size group do I feel the most comfortable and have the most success? Then seek those situations. Continue to try out the less comfortable situations too in order to expand your comfort zone.

> **One of the keys to effective networking is to understand group dynamics and recognize your position and status within each group.**

DYADS, TROIKAS, AND MINIS: THE SMALL GROUP NETWORKING EXPERIENCE

I don't know who originated the concept of breaking up into smaller groups for more in-depth networking, but it was a stroke of genius. There's only so much you can do in a large group. Discussions are often superficial, truncated, or drowned out by excessive ambient noise. The smaller follow-up meetings offer introverts and quieter people, who might be disadvantaged in the large group settings, a great opportunity for deeper, more intense discussions. The networking groups I'm currently involved in break people into small groups of three or four during the main large group meeting. The "troika" or "mini" members then decide on meeting for breakfast or lunch, a date, and a location. They could even decide to take a walk or meet at another novel location.

In any case, there are many forms the small group can take. Sometimes the individuals simply go around the table and talk more about the specifics of their business specialty and what kinds of referrals are useful to them. Other times people talk about current events, hobbies, children, or the networking process.

Every small group is different, for the chemistry and group dynamics shift with each configuration of people. We usually order food, and it's standard practice that the bill is evenly split, unless someone doesn't order anything or is a first-time guest to the networking organization. Some people insist on "picking up the tab," though that should not be an expectation.

Sometimes one individual takes charge of the troika or mini and might facilitate the discussion. In some cases one person dominates the conversation, and time runs out before all individuals have the opportunity to share about themselves. You can counter this tendency by gracefully asserting some time limits or redirecting the conversation. Some people need to be reminded of the importance of allowing everyone to speak. Often business is not discussed at all, especially when everyone knows the other people well. It can be a great time just to deepen the rapport and relationship and get to know more about people's background, education, and lives outside of business. However, the ultimate goal is usually about sharing business with one another, finding various gateways to people we want to meet, and increasing our knowledge base.

A large part of this process is based on intuition, emotional intelligence, and people skills. We're able to "go with the flow" in a small group situation. If everyone in the small group wants to talk about the Academy Awards and you want to talk about business, then you might need to wait until the group gets around to business talk. By realizing and accepting the fact that every group is a bit different, you'll learn how to adapt to the needs and interests of each group.

It's useful to find out about a person prior to the small group session by perusing their profile via their web sites or an Internet search. This will serve as preparation for the small group encounter. If the participants already know each other and are familiar with what everyone does, then referrals and advice can take place during these small group sessions. Some people are quite intentional in the small group meeting, and come prepared with names and contact numbers of people who could be useful to them. This practice is strongly recommended.

In general, the smaller the group is the more potential for deeper and more intimate communication. There's no doubt the dynamics of a small group changes as the size increases. However, as a group size increases, there are other advantages, like division of labor and more diverse ideas. Larger groups also give you the opportunity to observe people interacting with one another. Some groups are more open to new or additional members than others. It's useful to understand the advantages and disadvantages of small and large groups for different purposes other than networking. In fact, the addition or subtraction of one particular individual (such as a dominant one or one who doesn't fit in) can significantly alter the feel or dynamics of a small group.

Some people don't favor the random nature of troika assignments and opt to pre-select the people they'll meet with. They either request certain people to be assigned to, or avoid the troikas altogether.

Networking Tip - If you aren't comfortable at large group mixers, find someone you like and set up a one-on-one coffee meeting.

SOCIAL NORMS

Human beings in every culture have social norms that determine acceptable and unacceptable behavior and language. How we dress, how we speak, decorum, and what we talk about are all different from situation to situation. Different groups have various formats, guidelines and expectations that are usually determined by the organization or the leader of the group. When we join a group, we usually learn what is expected of us. What kind of clothes do we wear? What time do we show up? Is there a cost? Do we wear a name tag or badge?

We experience different norms in a classroom, a church, a bar, a party, or a board room. Sometimes we're given clear guidelines in the form of ground rules or a mission statement, or we might be instructed by a mentor. By listening and observing, we learn about the organization and decide to follow and adhere to the various social norms in different groups and situations.

There are different norms of social behavior, and they vary by region, socio-economic status, culture, age, profession, and situation. Touching, hugging, kissing, teasing, use of profanity, alcohol consumption, religious or political discussions, are all accepted or considered unacceptable in different situations and among different people. For example, it's quite common for Europeans to drink a glass of wine with lunch. However, today in many American settings it would be considered unusual. As we develop our emotional intelligence, we should be able to observe typical modes of behavior to have a good idea of acceptable behavior and language. I've noticed some conversations that start off formally and profanity-free, and end up riddled with profanity and off-color jokes as people get more comfortable with each other (or drink too much alcohol).

Norms have a strong regional, situational, and cultural component. The following are some examples:

- Wearing a cowboy hat is common in Texas, but unusual at a mixer in New York City.
- Men kissing each other as a greeting is common in Italy, but unusual in Ohio.
- A cocktail dress showing lots of cleavage is common at a Hollywood party, but uncommon at a Rotary Club in Kansas City.
- Profanity is normal at a comedy club, but unusual at a business meeting.
- Exchanging business cards is expected at a networking group, but not at a funeral.

In group networking, we need to learn the norms of each specific organization or group with which we're involved. Meeting format, speaking time, and attire are different from group to group. Norms lead to behavioral expectations in networking, such as giving referrals or leads, how we acknowledge others, and decorum during meetings or events.

In sum, there are normative behaviors for various situations. How we dress, what we say, how we pay a bill, and the length of meetings are all examples of commonly accepted norms within a situation. We're not *required* to follow established norms, but we are expected to do so.

DIFFERENCES AMONG GROUPS

Every group is different. It could be due to the influence of the leader, gender or ethnic demographics, the room setup, or a multitude of other factors. Some groups are quiet, some raucous, some are more cohesive, or contentious than others. As you network in a variety of settings (cross-networking), part of the fun is to notice the differences among the groups and how those differences affect group dynamics.

The leader can have a significant impact on the mood and feel of a particular group. The composition of the members is another major factor in large group dynamics. A group of all men is different from a group of all women. The same is true of homogeneous ages, ethnicity, and profession. As groups become more diverse, the dynamics are more difficult to predict. A New York state political caucus is different from a bingo game at a Jewish senior citizens' rest home in Brooklyn.

The demographics of groups have a significant impact on people's behavior within a given group. We might feel comfortable in a group of people of a similar age, gender, educational level, ethnicity, and socioeconomic level. Conversely, we might feel awkward or out of place with others who are from a different demographic group. It's useful to develop our comfort level with a variety of groups to enable us to network outside of our own "type." It helps us widen our sphere of influence to be flexible and versatile in our ability to relate to a wide variety of people. It's great to be comfortable with people who are similar to you, but it's also wise to expand your personal network by widening your horizons and contacts with people who might be different from you in gender, age, ethnicity, socioeconomic status, religion, and politics. It's useful to contact different types of people and to be versatile in your communication skills.

One of the fundamental principles in the psychology of networking is versatility, or getting along with a variety of people. The more diverse the people who know you and like you, the more success (and fun) you'll have networking. You should cultivate relationships with a diversity of people, occupations, and groups. For example, some people and groups like to talk about sports, politics, movies, or travel. A good conversationalist (and networker) feels comfortable in a variety of settings and groups.

THE PSYCHOLOGY OF CONFORMITY

People have a tendency to conform to certain standards of behavior. In a classic psychology study, Solomon Asch had subjects in his experiment look at a series of lines to determine which lines were the same length as others. Subjects were shown lines with obvious differences.

Shills who were part of the experimental team (not actual subjects but planted among them) began to give wrong answers. An interesting thing happened. **The subjects in the experiment, in the face of incorrect answers by others around them, actually went against their own judgment and gave wrong answers to conform to the group.** How we dress, where we place our name tag, and how we shake hands are all subject to group influence — that is, conformity to social norms. It is a norm in American business for men to shave prior to business meetings. However, in some settings and situations it might be acceptable for a male business person to go to a meeting unshaven, especially when we have observed others doing so.

There can be a strong social pressure to conform even in the face of our own discomfort. For example, if we go to a business lunch with three other people who order much more than we do, we might feel pressure to conform to the emerging norm of splitting the check equally despite the fact that we ordered very little or perhaps cannot afford as much. Our conformity in that situation is partially motivated by a desire to be accepted by the group and not to be perceived as miserly.

18

CONCLUSION

THIS book has given you all the tools you will need to become highly successful in your networking efforts. You'll build fruitful and mutually beneficial relationships that sometimes will be related to commerce and at other times will be more about friendship. At times you'll seek a friendship and get a business relationship out of it; other times you'll be looking for business and find a deep friendship. The two are intertwined.

This book's intention is to provide numerous ideas and specific techniques as a kind of "menu;" you can choose what you want and use it as you see fit. For example, you might not want to cross-network, and choose instead to focus all of your efforts on one single organization. You might choose a more traditional relationship-building approach or you might emphasize social media to expand and deepen your personal network. Your career, situation and personality will drive these decisions.

The business world will continue to change, especially as it relates to technology. Basic human interaction as we know it will become transformed in ways that are difficult to predict. Certain things, however, are immutable. Being a giver and trying to help others will continue to be more important than focusing on receiving referrals. Calling people by name, showing respect, under-standing personality differences, and making many "touches" (i.e., phone calls, e-mails, coffee or lunch meetings, sending birthday cards) will undoubtedly still be important many years from now. Technology and Internet networking will take on new dimensions. Networking web sites such as Twitter and LinkedIn are likely to proliferate. Some will thrive and others will fade away. But when all is said and done, there's still no substitute for face-to-face, person-to-person networking. You have to show up!

You're probably stronger in some areas. Some people are more intentional and regimented in networking than their peers. You can achieve success using various combinations of approaches. It's vitally important to be patient because successful networking takes time. If you do all of the things recommended in this book, on a consistent basis over a long period of time, you'll have an abundance of referrals and new business. Referrals and sales result more often from deeply developed and nurtured relationships than from on-the-fly encounters. **THEY DON'T HAPPEN OVERNIGHT!**

You don't have to throw dinner parties or have a regimented, specific program. You don't even have to do *everything* I suggest. The important thing is to understand the networking process as fully as possible and do as many of the things you can on a consistent basis. There are many unique recipes for success in learning effective networking skills. *It's up to you to determine exactly what to do and how frequently to do it.*

If you're more of an introvert, perhaps you'll do more online networking and less face-to-face "mixer" networking. Get to know yourself not only as you see yourself, but also as others perceive you. Be yourself and engage in activities you enjoy. Networking, though it does contain the word "work" in it, does not need to be work. It can and should be enjoyable. Mingling is an aspect of our social nature as humans, a way of being part of community and enjoying fellowship.

Your profession and the nature of your work will also influence how, when, and where you network. Some of your efforts will be profession-specific, while others will be more general. Networking might be a means to generate business or a vehicle for finding people to refer. It might even be a social vehicle. At times the results and value of your networking might be difficult to quantify. A relationship that began as purely business can turn into a friendship, and a friendship can develop into a business relationship. *You never know.*

As I reviewed my personal networking and relationship building experiences, interviews, and research for this book, certain principles emerged as being truths. It's crucial to give to others, not keep score, and if you do that generously and unselfishly you'll receive in return. It takes time to build solid personal and business relationships and these unfold in many different forms.

There's increasing empirical evidence that positive relationships can lead to a longer and happier life. So, whether or not you get business referrals and make more money as a consequence of effective networking, there's an inherent value in having numerous relationships. The true value of a relationship is impossible to measure. In his book *Man's Search for Meaning,* the Austrian psychologist Viktor Frankl argues that when all else is stripped away (as it was in the Nazi concentration camps where he was interned for a period of time), man searches for meaning somewhere, somehow. There are times when I so value a friendship I've forged through networking that the thought or prospect of business is not even on my "radar." I remember when I found out that Curt Castberg, whom I had met doing moves for UCLA in the 90s, had suffered a heart attack. I had really developed a friendship with Curt and was shocked, concerned, and saddened that he had such a close brush with death. It *meant* something to me. I was much more moved emotionally by that event than by losing or winning large business deals.

So, what, then, is the goal of networking? That depends. Sometimes, when business is slow, we're actively looking for leads and referrals. Other times we're open to meeting people to whom we can refer business or make introductions. But in many cases something happens that we didn't expect: a commonality, a shared hobby, an idea, or a friendship. A good friend of mine, Bud Backus, wrote a song with these memorable lyrics: "I searched for a penny, and I found a dime. I searched for a word and found a rhyme." Some people want to measure and predict everything and determine all conceivable outcomes in advance. Though that may be admirable and is a common practice, my experience informs me that YOU NEVER KNOW. People are akin to different chemicals, and you don't really know what will happen when you mix these elements together. Sometimes people assume because two individuals look alike and are both from the same geographic region that they will get along well. That may or may not be the case. It is the unpredictability of human behavior that makes it challenging and interesting.

I recommend an eclectic approach to networking that uses a combination of the ideas and techniques discussed in this book and elsewhere. More important, be yourself and use what works for you. If you don't like large groups, parties, or drinking, then nighttime mixers are not for you. If you function better in smaller groups, then set up those kinds of meetings and limit them to a few people. Do more of what you like to do and what works for you. The more enjoyment you get out of the networking process, the more benefits you'll gain, both personal and business. Remember the idea of the fisherman's net: it usually catches more kinds of fish than merely the ones intended.

I clearly remember working in my dad's toy store as a kid. He bought toys from a company called Federal Wholesale, which was owned by a Jewish family, the Bernsteins. He developed a wonderful friendship with the Bernsteins, especially the salesmen who called on our store, Bob Pennes and Jeff Miller. Christmas Eve was our busiest day of the year. Federal Wholesale, knowing we were very busy and didn't have time to cook or get dinner, would send us fantastic and memorable catered food from a delicatessen. Dad focused on his *relationship* with Bob and Jeff, and nurtured it. It provided meaning. I attended his children's Bar Mitzvot and they attended my sisters' weddings. In a real sense, we were part of each other's family. We usually don't go into networking looking for people to attend our family's weddings or Bar Mitzvot. But we do end up building relationships that become much more than we ever expected — adding pleasure, meaning, and prosperity to our life.

The BOTTOM LINE is this: Do what works for you, as much or as little as you want to do it! If you enjoy an organization so much that you get totally involved in your own club, that may be enough of a networking program for you. You might only be interested in developing your business. Or perhaps you may end up developing a number of wonderful and long-lasting friendships. There are innumerable paths to success and enjoyment through diverse types of networking events, organizations, and venues.

This book does not offer you a specific program or script to be memorized. It's about becoming more of yourself in communion with others. Every successful person I interviewed had a slightly different perception of the networking process. There were common themes such as: give and focus on giving rather than on receiving, be likeable, follow up, do an outstanding job, be respectful of others, and show up. But beyond those and a few others, all successful profiles represented some variation on the wide theme of getting involved, caring about others as much as yourself, and remembering that we're all part of a social process that weaves our personal and professional lives into a beautiful tapestry.

PART 5

APPENDICES

APPENDIX A:
NETWORKING DIARY

T*his section presents an actual diary of my current networking experiences, sometimes focusing on a specific day, sometimes a week, sometimes a longer period of time. This diary will allow you to see exactly what activities were performed and what results were achieved. The actual names have been omitted to protect identities.*

My networking schedule is more rigorous and varied than most people. I have the time, the inclination, and the circumstances that allow this to occur. You don't have to follow my schedule in order to be successful, but it's useful to have a varied and strategic program for maximal success. It's imperative to be consistent, to leverage your various connections, and to deepen your existing relationships. Get involved in the various groups you belong to. Call people by name and build on the information you learn about people. Do more than you think you should do, and the results will be bountiful.

WEEK 1

Monday: Monday was a national holiday, Presidents' Day, and my 60th birthday. I didn't network.

Tuesday: I attended a morning meeting of ProVisors as a guest. Lunch was a troika from a prior ProVisors meeting. I sent approximately 25 network-related e-mails.

Wednesday: I attended a morning Bruin Professionals meeting where I was the speaker on networking. In the evening I attended a mixer for IFMA, the facility manager trade organization. I sent 20 e-mails.

Thursday: I attended a morning ProVisors meeting as a guest, where I received a public testimonial extolling the virtues of my company. In the evening I attended another IFMA event (different chapter and more cross-networking). Both events were very productive for me and I met several potential clients.

Friday: I attended a breakfast meeting for the Executive Committee of my home ProVisors group. Seven people attended, and it was a work meeting. I then visited the offices of some people whom I had met at the Wednesday IFMA event, and learned more about their business. My lunch was a follow-up troika from a ProVisors meeting. I sent 15 networking e-mails.

Comments on the week: I must begin eating healthier at these networking meals, but bacon is so tempting. Every meeting is like a snowflake, different one from another. You never know what will be discussed, or what chemistry might or might not exist. The highlights were the public testimonial (by a well-connected member of ProVisors) and the IFMA events, where I met a number of potential clients.

WEEK 2

Monday: I started this week with a pleasant breakfast ProVisors troika. There were two other people, one a lawyer and the other a financial planner. I not only talked about my moving business, but also discussed this book and my upcoming speaking engagements. The chemistry of this troika was great.

Tuesday: The morning began with a large group Real Estate affinity group of ProVisors, attended by numerous commercial real estate brokers. It was productive for me. In the evening I met with a move consultant I've worked with on several occasions. We discussed both business and our personal backgrounds.

Wednesday: I was the featured speaker at my home group of ProVisors. The presentation went very well. For lunch, I attended a committee meeting for my local IFMA chapter. One of the attendees handles facilities for a large local university. Though we focused on our agenda, I did exchange business cards with that person, and let it be known that I would be interested in future moving business. This meeting was an example of getting involved, and how sometimes we can best meet decision makers by our involvement.

Thursday: I attended the monthly morning meeting of Downtown Bruin

Professionals. I ran one segment of that meeting and will be speaking to that group next month.

Friday: I took the day off to prepare for my 60th birthday party. This was a networking-free day.

Comments on the week: This week involved a few key networking principles. This first was the importance of getting involved. The second underscores the value of public speaking. I did "passive networking" as the true nexus of my 60th birthday party with 50+ attendees. I did no business networking at that event, but the 50 closest people to me represent a substantial and significant part of my network.

WEEK 3

Monday: Sent 25 e-mails. No networking events were attended.

Tuesday: Attended an afternoon cocktail meeting with a client and building manager.

Wednesday: Spoke to a chapter meeting of Bruin Professionals on business networking. Attended an evening event for the UCLA Real Estate group.

Thursday: No networking events.

Friday: Attended a ProVisors meeting in Pasadena. It was a friendly group, and I met a very well-connected commercial real estate broker who plans to attend my upcoming presentation on business networking.

Comments on the week: This week saw the blending of my speaking engagements, cross-networking, and making some great contacts. The more I attend various meetings as a guest, the more of an overall nexus I become in ProVisors. After attending a few times, some members of a particular chapter think I'm a member of that chapter. It's all about fitting in. When you get to that point of fitting in, networking gets easier and even becomes effortless. We find a home in a group.

WEEK 4

Monday: Attended a troika breakfast for Bruin Professionals.

Tuesday: Took a building manager to lunch and discussed the tenant configuration of her building and possible upcoming moves.

Wednesday: Had a breakfast troika and only one guy showed up. He's a veteran business broker and mentored me on my career. It's unlikely that

I can refer business to him, so the mentoring/trusted advisor role suited him well.

Thursday: Had a breakfast meeting with a guy to discuss how to derive maximal benefit from LinkedIn. He later gave me a referral for a move.

Friday: No networking events.

Comments on the week: This was a relatively light networking week, but I did make a couple of strong and meaningful connections.

WEEK 5

Monday: Attended a troika breakfast for Bruin Professionals. This was a positive and enjoyable group of three people. I learned something interesting at this meeting, that some lawyers in very large national firms don't refer business to lawyers outside of their firm. This explains why there are not many of these large national firm attorneys in networking groups. After this breakfast meeting I met a business writer for coffee to discuss her business and possible networking.

Tuesday: Attended a chapter meeting for Bruin Professionals. I'm Speaker Chair for this particular chapter and I read the Mission Statement at every meeting. I'm visible and attend regularly. Being Speaker Chair, people call me to try to get booked as a speaker, and that puts me more in the nexus position for this chapter. I noticed two people dozing off during the meeting. One of them rarely attends, does not participate much, and leaves early. The leader has attended one of the highest number of total meetings of any member (they do keep records on such things). He also is a leader in many UCLA-related groups and clubs, and a huge UCLA sports fan. I sent four LinkedIn invitations to new people I met there, and received two "acceptances" the same day. There was a discussion after the meeting about the qualifications for becoming a member, one of which is seven years of experience in a profession. Some debated the soundness of this rule. After the meeting, I visited a building manager where I'm doing a move, and got better acquainted with her.

Wednesday: Guested at another chapter of ProVisors. It was the first time I attended this particular chapter. The group was raucous, there was a lot of joking and teasing, and irreverence. I think it's interesting to notice the range in groups in terms of behavior and seriousness. This group obviously likes to have fun, and has built a certain reputation on their behvavior. I met some new people, and ended up in a troika with two people whose business partners I already knew from other networking experiences. That evening I attended a networking event for Association of Legal Administrators at the House of Blues in Hollywood. I ran into several people I know, some I had done business with, and some new people. I made at least one solid contact with someone who might utilize my services in the near future.

Thursday: I guested at another chapter of ProVisors and made a couple of strong contacts, one with a commercial real estate broker whom I had met on another occasion. On the way back to the office, I stopped at two buildings and talked to the building managers.

Friday: I began the day having coffee with a major commercial broker in Glendale. I had originally met him when I guested at another chapter of ProVisors after someone recommended that I attend that chapter because that broker was a member. He subsequently heard my presentation on networking. Our meeting was very friendly and productive. He gave me two solid referrals, and booked me to speak to his entire brokerage staff on networking. The net result is that I'm getting moving referrals and am increasing my exposure to networking audiences through this connection. I also attended a ProVisors networking luncheon, where I met some new people and sat at a table with people I already knew and deepened that relationship. In all, it was a fruitful day and week. My LinkedIn Connections went from 525 to 540 this week and are growing continually.

WEEK 6

Monday: I began the week with a Mini (troika) of my Westwood Chapter of Bruin Professionals. There were four of us, and we each talked a bit about our business. One participant was surprised when I explained that my company did a lot of on-premise moving for companies remodeling, painting, or carpeting instead of relocating.

Tuesday: Attended as a guest of another ProVisors group. The more I guest, the more comfortable I feel, especially when I know and like a few people in the groups at which I'm guesting.

Wednesday: Attended a chapter of Bruin Professionals with only 9 attendees. I did get to know one new person at that meeting.

Thursday: Guested at a ProVisors meeting, and was able to talk a bit about my work on networking.

Friday: No networking, as I took the day off.

NOTE: Every meeting is different. It's useful to be flexible; sometimes you'll lead the discussion and other times you'll follow, depending on your position and status in a particular group. Continually work on developing and deepening existing relationships. Don't prejudge others or their potential value to you before you've had the opportunity to speak with them. You might be surprised, as I have been on many occasions.

APPENDIX B: ORGANIZING A COLLEGE/FRATERNITY REUNION

I attended a small Catholic men's college called University of San Diego (USD) between the years 1966 and 1968 for my freshman and sophomore years. I was part of a fraternity called Tau Kappa Epsilon (TKE), and made a number of friends during those years. For the most part I lost contact with those friends, with a few exceptions.

I do have one very strong USD contact, my boss and mentor, Larry Whittet, who was a year behind me and also a TKE member. When I went to work at a company called Western Mayflower in 1983, Larry was Vice President of that company, and we reconnected and have been in touch since then. Another TKE, Phil Pirio, found me at a book signing I was doing in Pasadena in the mid 1990s. By bits and pieces I had seen a few classmates and fraternity brothers over the years, but my stronger connection had always been with UCLA, where I received two degrees.

Earlier last year another TKE member, Larry Flores, had a 60th birthday party and I attended. During that party I became reacquainted with a number of my USD classmates, most of whom were also TKEs. The idea of a reunion was bantered about, and I took it on myself to be the organizer.

This is when it got interesting for me. I gradually became the nexus of the reunion, even though I didn't even graduate from USD or stay involved with the fraternity members over the years. I tended to get along with most everyone, was primarily responsible for finding people, and learned the various spheres of influence. In general, people only stayed connected with a couple or a few others. Not everyone liked everyone else or had much of a connection with many people.

I became the nexus primarily because I had contact with a large number of people and built relationships with graduates from various years. My position of reunion organizer also hastened that change from two year transferee to nexus.

The reunion itself was a huge success, attended by a large majority of invitees. Old friendships were rekindled and a new wave of communication among the fraternity members flourished. It was much better attended than I imagined and the varied results of our organizational efforts continue to reverberate among the "brothers."

APPENDIX C: SPECIFIC NETWORKING ORGANIZATIONS: DESCRIPTIONS AND MISSIONS

This section will describe in more detail two networking and professional groups that have been utilized in this book for examples. There are many more like them, and these are just a couple of examples.

PROVISORS

ProVisors was established in Los Angeles, California in 1988 as Professionals Network Group, Inc. The founders are Davis Blaine and Gordon Gregory. Originally it was not designed as a networking organization but rather as an assembly of "deal makers" and "trusted advisors" who had been working together. Deal makers would utilize the group to clear the details of their pending deals. It was established to provide a community for professionals who believe that success flows from a commitment to high ethical standards and to a devotion to the best interest of clients by sharing resources and knowledge with fellow senior professionals. Over time it has expanded and developed to over 1,300 professional members throughout California with plans for nationwide expansion.

> **The mission statement**: "ProVisors is a community of professionals who serve their clients as trusted advisors and share the highest standards of integrity, performance and accountability. ProVisors promotes and enables relationship building, information sharing, and collaboration among its members for the benefit of their clients and one another."

Membership in ProVisors is by **invitation only.** The standards are stringent, and the membership is comprised primarily of business professionals. There's a large representation by attorneys, accountants, bankers, insurance professionals, a variety of financial professionals, business consultants, real estate professionals, sole practitioners, and business coaches. Membership is limited to respected professionals and trusted advisors with an established "book of business." Each geographic chapter is responsible for qualifying and inviting people to join. The chapter's leader and executive committee make that decision to extend an invitation after meeting prospective members.

ProVisors focuses on higher level, well-established professionals. Every chapter is managed differently. Some follow a strict format, while others are less structured, based upon preference of the group leader. The meetings are held monthly in the conference rooms of the host/sponsor from 7 a.m. to 9 a.m. Guesting is strongly encouraged so you can meet people who are not members of your home chapter.

Additionally, there are a number of so-called "affinity groups" with a specialized focus, such as: Entertainment, Technology, Non-Profit, Cross-Cultural Business, Distributors and Manufacturers, and Real Estate. There are frequent mixers and joint chapter meetings, educational programs, and luncheons, and an annual Holiday Mixer. Gordon Gregory describes ProVisors as a *community*.

ProVisors is a dynamic organization that generates a huge amount of commerce through referrals, introductions, and strategic alliances. ProVisors has an outstanding web site that regularly announces jobs, business opportunities, member needs, and upcoming events.

BRUIN PROFESSIONALS

Bruin Professionals, or BP as it is known and "branded," is a UCLA alumni networking organization established in 2003. BP is the premier networking organization for UCLA alumni and focuses on "Building Business Between Bruins." There are currently chapters in Westwood, Encino, Pasadena, Downtown Los Angeles, Orange County, San Diego and the South Bay area. It's open to any UCLA alum with at least seven years as an established and seasoned professional.

> **The mission statement**: "The mission of Bruin Professionals (BP) is to assemble a diverse group of UCLA Alumni who are well established in a profession or business and are willing to make a commitment to attend BP meetings. BP members will have the opportunity through

an organized format to develop relationships and expand their business activities by sharing referrals, resources, information, ideas, and advice. BP will develop Bruin synergy and establish a venue through which professional Alumni can become actively associated with UCLA and promote new business leads."

The main goal of BP is to increase commerce among Bruins by the sharing of referrals, resources, advice, and business information. Each chapter meets once a month, followed by a BP mini, a randomly designated 3 to 4 people who meet for breakfast or lunch following a chapter meeting. The chapters are comprised of a wide variety of professionals such as attorneys, accountants, financial professionals, consultants, and experts in real estate, insurance, and other fields.

In addition to the chapter meetings and minis, there's a web site and BP Exchange which allows the posting of needs, deals, wants, and other pertinent information. The main chapter meetings take place one morning a month (for example on the third Wednesday of every month) from 7 a.m. until 9 a.m. in the boardroom of the sponsoring host. Every attendee gets the opportunity to give a 60 second "elevator speech" to highlight their business, area of expertise, and what a good referral would be for them. The chapter meetings begin with open networking (mixing and mingling), and food and beverages are provided. There's normally a speaker on a topic of interest to the members.

It is recommended that members attend more than one chapter meeting if it fits into their schedule (cross-networking). BP's purpose includes providing a directory of service professionals to the UCLA community at large.

APPENDIX D:
REFERRAL ETIQUETTE

Wherever and however you end up networking, it's important to be courteous and respectful in relation to giving and receiving referrals. I recommend following these basic principles:

- Thank the person who provides you with a referral.
- Respond promptly to every referral.
- When you set an appointment, be sure to confirm it a day or two before the meeting.
- Show up on time.
- Be prepared for all meetings and discussions.
- Keep the person who gave you the referral "in the loop" and informed of the status and progress of the "deal."
- Be professional at all times.
- Perform an outstanding job to demonstrate your worthiness to receive the referral.
- Never say anything derogatory about the person who gave you the referral.
- Try to reciprocate with a referral to the person who referred you.
- Always be sure to return to the original source of referral for any possible cross-referrals.

APPENDIX E: ADDITIONAL NETWORKING GUIDELINES

This is a book about *professional* networking and relationship building. It's vitally important to be a professional in all aspects of networking. Establish clear boundaries when necessary, such as times of availability for business and topics of discussion. If you have strong political or religious beliefs, you need to determine if you want to share them with your business associates.

Show respect for others at all times! Do what you say you're going to do when you say you're going to do it. Keep confidential information private, and follow professional and legal guidelines.

Another important issue in networking is behaving ethically. Be honest, have integrity, and treat others fairly. Always engage in professional business behavior.

Do not dismiss people you don't initially like. More important, don't speak ill of or gossip about others. Sometimes those we don't initially like turn out to become great resources and even friends. A good rule to follow is this: If you don't have anything good to say about someone, don't say anything at all.

APPENDIX F:
PLACES TO NETWORK

Y ou can network almost anywhere. However, the following places are the most optimal:

- Mixers
- Networking Functions
- Conventions
- Trade Shows
- Conferences
- Business Meetings
- Networking Groups
- Service Clubs like Rotary, Lions, Elks and Kiwanis
- Social Clubs
- Trade Organization Meetings
- Athletic Activities like Golf or Softball
- Organization Committees
- Alumni Organizations
- PTA Meetings
- Restaurants, Bars and Clubs
- Chambers of Commerce
- Toastmasters
- Airports and Airplanes
- Social Events
- Sporting Events
- Business Events
- Cultural Events
- Parties
- Shows

- Seminars
- Civic Organizations
- Volunteer Organizations
- Church Groups
- Schools and Educational Events
- Charity Organizations
- Private Clubs like Yacht or Tennis Clubs
- Health Clubs
- Dog Parks
- Social Media Sites like Linkedin and Plaxo

APPENDIX G:
KEY NETWORKING TIPS
TO REMEMBER

The following tips will lead you to successful business networking:

- Listen more than you speak. Be constantly aware if you have a tendency to dominate a conversation.
- Make an effort to establish some common ground with the person you're talking with. When someone mentions a topic you know something about or are interested in, try to make an appropriate connection.
- When you're face-to-face with two people who don't know each other, make an introduction.
- Make an **effort** to connect people, and to respond to others' needs, deals, and wants.
- Take a leap of faith and make that referral after developing some level of confidence in the person to whom you're referring.
- Try to get to know people by asking open-ended, interested questions.
- Try to help others as much as you can, rather than focusing on what you're receiving. **Don't keep score**! Be a giver, not a taker.
- Stay in touch with people through e-mail, phone calls, or mailers.
- Find the center of influence (nexus) in a group and build a relationship with that person. Ideally, become a nexus and center of influence yourself.
- Don't make too many assumptions about a person's potential value as a networking source or partner. You never know.
- Cross-network and use old relationships to establish new ones.
- Be patient waiting for referrals, but if the time is right, ask for one.

- Don't always ask the same questions or tell the same stories. Be both interested and interesting.
- Blend business with a personal touch, whether it's about children, animals, or common interests.
- Stayin touch with classmates, business associates, and friends.
- Plumb your own network to assist others in their various needs.
- Try to remember what people say to you so you can continue a train of thought rather than starting from scratch every time you see them.
- Be likable and genuine. You're more likely to get referrals if people like you and like to be around you.
- Pay attention to people and don't interrupt them or cut them off in mid-thought or mid-sentence.
- Always thank people promptly and follow up on EVERY referral. Above all, do an outstanding job and make yourself valuable to others.

BIBLIOGRAPHY

Acuff, Jerry. *The Relationship Edge*. Hoboken, NJ: John Wiley and Sons, Inc., 2007.

Asher, Joey. *Selling and Communication Skills for Lawyers*. New York: ALM Publishing, 2005.

Burg, Bob. *Endless Referrals* (3rd Edition). New York: McGraw-Hill, 2005.

Bjorseth, Lillian D. *Breakthrough Networking: Building Relationships that Last*. Lisle, IL: Duoforce Press, 2003.

Ferrazzi, Keith. *Never Eat Alone*. New York: Doubleday, 2005.

Fine, Debra. *The Fine Art of Small Talk*. New York: Hyperion Press, 2005.

Fisher, Donna and Sandy Vilas. *Power Networking*. Austin: Bard Press, 2000.

Frankl, Viktor. Man's Search for Meaning. Boston: Beacon Press, 1963.

Fraser, George C. *Click*. New York: McGraw Hill, 2008.

Gitomer, Jeffrey. *Little Black Book of Connections*. Austin: Bard Press, 2006.

Harris, Thomas. *I'm OK — You're OK*. Harper Collins, 1969.

Mackay, Harvey. *Dig Your Well Before You're Thirsty*. New York: Doubleday, 1990.

Nierenberg, Andrea. *Nonstop Networking: How to Improve your Life, Luck and Career*. Sterling, VA: Capital Books, 2002.

Saleebey, William M. *Sell Yourself*. Santa Monica: Mentor Publishing, 1994.

Salmon, Michael. *Super Networking*. Franklin Lakes: Career Press, 2004.

Savar, Sheila. *The Power of Networking*. Reston, VA: Bama Press, 2008.

Templeton, Tim. *The Referral of a Lifetime*. San Francisco: Berrett-Koehler Publisher, 2005.

Tieger, Paul D. and Barbara Barron-Tieger. *Just Your Type*. New York: Little, Brown, and Company, 2000.

INDEX